SPONSOR MAGNET

How to attract, price, & execute your
dream brand partnerships

Hey there,

Thank you for picking up my book! I completely wrung my brain to teach you everything I know about brand sponsorships so it's wild and ridiculously fulfilling you're holding these pages.

Here's the deal: you can get all the bonuses I mention in the rest of this book for FREE by scanning the QR code or going to this link: sponsormagnet.com/bonus

All right, it's time to transform you into a Sponsor Magnet. Ready?

—Justin

ISBN: 979-8-9911630-6-4

T I L T
PUBLISHING

Tilt Publishing
700 Park Offices Drive, Suite 250
Research Triangle, NC 27709

JUSTIN MOORE

SPONSOR MAGNET

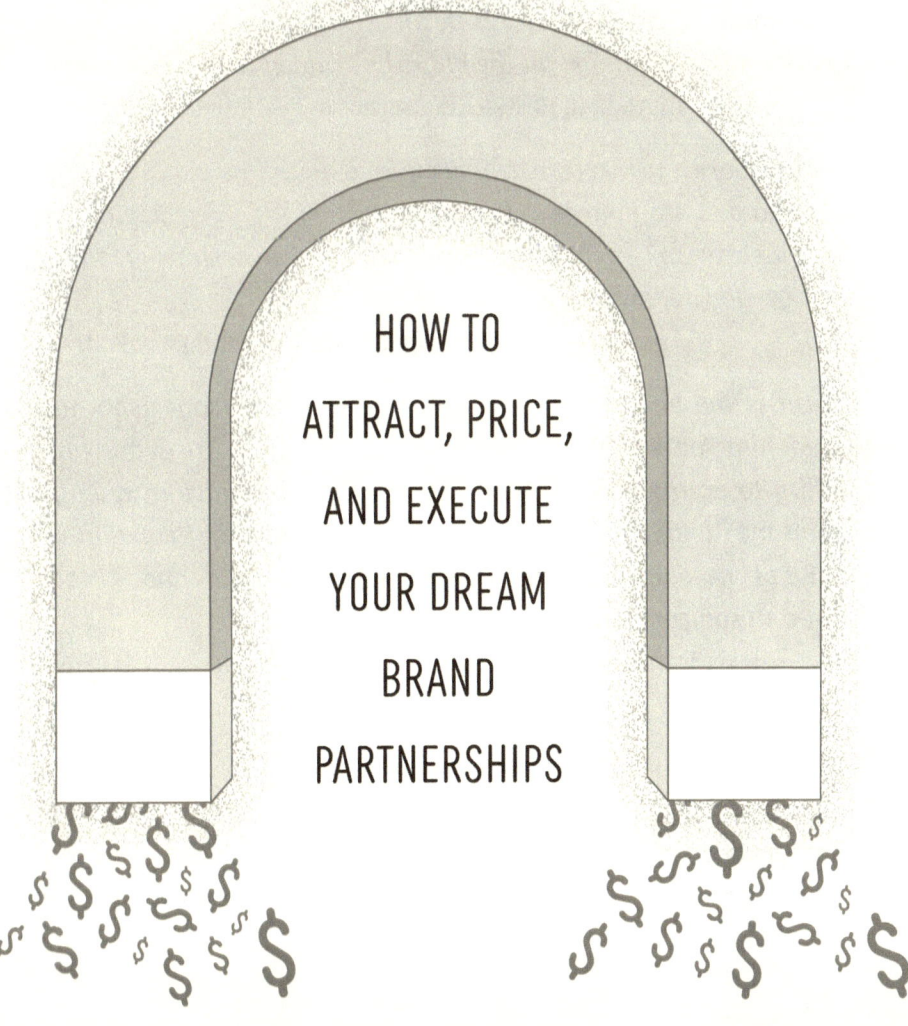

HOW TO
ATTRACT, PRICE,
AND EXECUTE
YOUR DREAM
BRAND
PARTNERSHIPS

There is one person on the planet I trust for sponsorship advice, and it's Justin Moore. In fact, I did trust him for advice, and it doubled my sponsorship revenue in the next six months.

—Jay Clouse, Creator Science

Sponsor Magnet is an invaluable resource. There are so many moving parts in managing sponsorships. I wish every creator would read this book—it'd make my job easier and speed up the time between booking and payment.

—Justine Galea, Partnerships at Kit

We've had an almost 2X increase in the sponsorship revenue we've made to the tune of £200,000...we owe a lot of money to Justin and his team for all the value he's added to our business.

—Ali Abdaal, Best-selling author of Feel Good Productivity

Justin Moore and his team helped me land a six-figure sponsorship and showed me how to position myself as the perfect partner for big brands. They made navigating sponsorships a game-changer for my business.

—Paul Jamison, Green Industry Podcast

Justin is the brand sponsorship wizard. As someone who has hired him for several campaigns, his attention to detail and ability to create something really creative and custom always blows me away. Sponsor Magnet will help you gain the valuable insights necessary to be a successful partner and create win-win solutions.

—Alexis Teichmiller, Senior Brand Partnerships Manager at Circle

We're living at the start of a new era in media – when so much of the attention and influence is flowing from traditional advertising to independent creators pursuing their passion on the Internet. The money is starting to follow, and there's no one better positioned at the edge of that wave than Justin Moore. By following his advice we've 5x'd our sponsorship revenue, which has opened up completely new business models and opportunities for us. There's no one I recommend more to help you understand how to partner with the world's most important companies in mutually beneficial ways that grow your bottom line while also funding your art, your ideas, and your contributions as a creator.

—Tiago Forte, Best-selling author of *Building a Second Brain*

Justin's advice single-handedly helped me quit my 9-to-5 job. I was able to find and negotiate my dream partnership to successfully replace my salary for an entire year. It's about time the rest of the world gets access to Justin's genius!

—Molly Donlan, Demystify Magic Podcast

It's about time somebody wrote THE BOOK on sponsorships, and there's no one more qualified and trustworthy to write this book than Justin. He's helped countless people generate more revenue authentically and Sponsor Magnet should be in every personal brand and marketer's library.

—Pat Flynn, Smart Passive Income

Justin Moore's guidance was the key that unlocked the door to brand sponsorships for me. His strategies opened up a whole new income stream, allowing me to turn my passion into a thriving business beyond my 9-5 job.

—Dr. Aleksandra Zuraw, Digital Pathology Place

As an agent, manager, and marketer who has overseen 8 figures plus in sponsorships, I can say with the utmost confidence that Justin Moore's work in this book is not just recommended reading - it is mandatory. With his signature, passion-filled style of prose, Justin gives you immediate access to the tools you need to make your sponsorship dreams come true.

—Kevin Herrera, The Machine

There are a lot of people out there giving advice about sponsorships but nobody can help you like Justin can. He's not only as experienced as it gets on the subject of brand deals but he communicates what he knows in a way that anyone can understand. Sponsor Magnet is your gateway to making real money from your content.

—Nick Nimmin, YouTube educator

Since connecting with Justin, we've unlocked opportunities we never imagined! In less than a year, we generated six figures in sponsorship and brand deals - all through partnerships that align perfectly with our values and vision and authentic campaigns that genuinely resonated with us and our audience. Justin and his team have helped us do far more than increase revenue; they've helped us create meaningful, long-term relationships with brands that not only see our value but truly view us as partners.

—Jessica DiPietro & Christian Manhard, Moose Painting

Justin is the go-to person for sponsorship advice and strategy, and the only person I trust. His exact strategies have generated my business multiple six figures in revenue, and brands now consistently tell me I'm the best creator they've ever worked with.

—Logan Nathanson, Favorite Finds

Justin Moore is the leading expert in sponsorships and long-term brand partnerships. He has sat in every chair in this arena and has deeper knowledge of it than anyone else in our industry. Sponsor Magnet is the definitive textbook for anyone looking to increase their income as a creator, and is required reading.

—Roberto Blake, Awesome Creator Academy

To my wife, April, for leading the way.

Table of Contents

Becoming a Sponsor Magnet

"We have a serious problem," the ad agency executive says. "Your contract has an error and the brand isn't sure if we can proceed with the shoot tomorrow."

My stomach drops. A sudden jolt as the airplane pushes back from the gate.

"What do you mean?" I say into the phone, trying to tune out a passenger yapping loudly in the row behind me. "You realize that we're about to take off?"

I look over at my wife, April, trying to soothe our two-year-old son on her lap.

She mouths, "What are they saying?"

I shake my head in disbelief. Our five-year-old son sitting between us was, thankfully, distracted by a show on his tablet.

For a moment, I think about pulling up the sponsorship contract on my phone and trying to figure out which clause had the issue.

I glance up and see a flight attendant staring daggers at me.

Think, Justin, think.

The plane begins its wide turn onto the runway.

There was no time. It was impossible.

There was only one clause I could see clearly in my mind:

Compensation: $25,000.

My heart was in my throat as I thought of everything we were hoping to use that money for: mortgage payments, bills, that vacation I had promised to April.

Were we really about to lose it all?

I've been in high-stakes situations with brands many times before.

In fact, today, I'm the guy hundreds of top creators and businesses call when they need help negotiating complex five- and six-figure sponsorships.

But I wasn't always that guy.

Back in 2009, the only thing I was good at negotiating was...free stuff.

April and I were fresh out of college with our first full-time jobs, barely making enough to afford a small apartment together.

When we would get home from work, our idea of a good time was to drive to our local thrift store and see if we could find anything valuable to flip on eBay.

April would consistently find designer jeans for $10-15 and later sell them for $50.

I, on the other hand, loved hunting for priceless art and sculptures that I imagined someone accidentally donated while cleaning out their attic. Turns out most attic cleaners also had access to something called the "Internet." Who knew? I settled for flipping old textbooks.

The extra cash was fun but nothing life-changing.

To be honest, we didn't think of ourselves as side-hustlers or entrepreneurs.

We were just normal people, with normal jobs and a normal life.

But one day, I was lying on the couch in our apartment watching a YouTube video while April did her makeup next to me.

"You should start a makeup channel," I told her. "You're good at that stuff."

"I don't know," she said. "Isn't YouTube just a bunch of cat videos?"

"There *are* a lot of cat videos," I said. "But there's also people doing makeup tutorials, skits, and other cool things."

She was skeptical. "Maybe. But how would we film it?"

"I have that old camcorder," I said. "I'll even help you edit the video on Windows Movie Maker. I made a slideshow using that in college one time."

She shrugged, then broke into a smile.

It was settled.

That weekend, April filmed her very first YouTube video in the bathroom of our tiny little apartment.

She showed people how to use a coiled spring called Bellabe to remove facial hair (yes, it's as painful as it sounds).

I took the footage, added some terrible neon pink and green title graphics, and hit upload.

The first day, her video got 23 views.

She was shocked. She didn't even have 23 friends in real life, let alone 23 people who would be interested in this bizarre hair removal technique.

But after *thirty* days, 3,721 people had watched the video, including...someone from the brand.

Not long after, Bellabe emailed April, thanking her profusely and offering to send her more products (for free) if she talked about them again.

Incredulous, she gladly accepted their offer.

My contribution to this first "negotiation?" Absolutely nothing. I thought it was awesome! Who doesn't love free stuff?

So, April started filming and uploading videos consistently.

And *more* brands started reaching out with *more* free products in exchange for promotion.

"Sure, send them over!" was the universal answer.

By 2010, I had enrolled in a part-time MBA program at night after work.

I started taking marketing, sales, and negotiation classes, and my gears started turning.

April was constantly getting comments on her videos like:

"Wow, I've never heard of this brand!"

"Thanks, I just bought it on their site!"

"Just went to the store and got it. Thanks for the tip!"

The more I thought about the value she was providing to these brands, the more I felt that "free stuff" was kind of a raw deal.

So, when the next brand emailed April, I told her to ask them what their collaboration budget was.

"There's no way anyone will pay me *money*," she said.

"Just try it," I said.

Soon, an online skincare store called iMomoko reached out.

"Do you have a budget for collaborating with me?" she emailed back.

"Sure, if you can include us in two videos a month, we'll pay you $700 monthly."

We were stunned.

$700 was a massive chunk of our rent at the time!

April turned to me and said, "Can you handle these brand emails from now on?"

Back to the airplane.

"It's the clause about the deliverables," the ad exec said. "There was a miscommunication internally. We screwed up, and the version of the contract we sent you should have included a video, not just social media posts. The problem is that we don't have any budget flex. And the video is what the brand has its heart set on."

The picture was becoming clearer. This error wasn't our fault, but that didn't change the fact that the deal was in jeopardy.

I took a deep breath and said calmly, "Look, we're about to take off and don't land until late. The call time for the shoot tomorrow is 4:30 a.m. You're correct that adding a video into the scope would require more compensation, but there's no way we can figure this out right now. Can you tell the brand they have our word that we'll all sit together after the shoot to find a compromise that works for everyone?"

Silence on the line for a few moments.

"OK, I'll tell the brand that we can proceed with the shoot."

Most people approach problems during negotiations from a "winner-takes-all" perspective.

But that rarely leads to a positive outcome. Sure, you may maximize your revenue in the short term, but the likelihood of getting repeat business from that company is now near zero.

Instead, if you can empathize with them and understand that they're real people with their own motivations, hopes, and fears, finding a mutually beneficial compromise becomes the clear goal.

Had we refused to play ball and the brand lost a bunch of money on a canceled shoot because the ad exec screwed up the contract, would the agency lose the entire account? Would that exec lose her bonus? Get passed over for a promotion? *Get fired?*

The opposite happened in real life. The shoot went amazing. We agreed to add the video but *reduced* the number of social media posts. The brand was thrilled and the exec was a hero. And surprise, surprise: over the next few years, that agency brought us several more five-figure sponsorships.

This long-term view of partnerships always felt obvious. My goal was never to make the most money possible on each deal but rather to increase the number of times each client hired us. I figured we'd make more money and attract sponsors like a magnet if we became their favorite people to work with.

But whenever I told our creator friends that April and I had done 550 sponsorships, earning over $5,000,000, they were shocked.

"How are you getting that many deals?" they'd say.

"Tell me about your pitching strategy," I'd say back, usually met with blank stares.

"Pitching strategy? I don't pitch brands. I'm just focusing on growing my audience, and sometimes brands reach out to collaborate," they'd say.

"How often are brands reaching out?" I'd ask.

"It's unpredictable. Some months there are a bunch, and some months almost none," they'd answer.

First red flag.

"OK, but when they *do* reach out, how do you calculate how much to charge?" I'd say.

"I usually just ask my friends if they've ever worked with that company and how much they charged."

Second red flag.

"Hmm. How often are brands hiring you again after the first partnership?" I'd then ask.

"Rarely. Every deal I do feels like a one-off 'transaction,' and the brand never reaches out again."

That's three red flags, if you're counting.

I began to realize that April and I were doing something... *different.*

You might think you know what happened next:

> *Justin starts a business managing other creators and uses his methodologies to help them get sponsorships (for a cut).*

But that's *not* what happened.

I sensed a more significant opportunity.

See, becoming a manager, agent, or broker never interested me.

Two reasons:
1. April and I had awful experiences with managers early on in our journey
2. My friends who *were* managers constantly complained about how needy their clients were

No, thanks.

I had a *better* idea.

The brands and companies that kept hiring April and me over and over always told us the same thing: "We love working with you because it's seamless. You always deliver stuff on time. We rarely need revisions on what you deliver. And you're polite."

I wondered...could I charge a fee for *that* "service," help brands execute more extensive campaigns, and get more sponsorships for our friends?

After all, brands have the money; why not go straight to the source?

It sure felt like a good business model.

I decided to shoot my shot.

April had just finished a brand partnership facilitated by a large public relations agency, so I emailed them and said, "This was such a great campaign! Are you looking for additional family-friendly creators to partner with? We have a bunch of friends with sizable audiences and I can help you collaborate with them as well."

The agency was intrigued.

Turns out finding good partners was a significant pain point for them.

Many others I pitched shared the same frustrations.

Here's how their outreach would usually go down:
- 50% of creators would never respond
- 25% would take at least a week to respond
- 15% would respond promptly but couldn't participate due to schedule conflicts or other obligations
- 5% would respond promptly and be available (but charge too much)
- 5% would respond promptly and be available (and within budget)

Plus, when brands *were* able to forge partnerships, the vast majority of folks were unprofessional, slow to respond, and delivered sub-par work.

Not ideal.

So, I pitched *more* brands.

In every conversation, I learned something new:
- How advertising budgets are set and approved internally

- Why brands often don't care about audience size
- Why they rarely respond to cold pitches
- How they audit the online presence of prospective partners
- Why they choose to hire some partners again and put others on a list called "NEVER WORK WITH THIS PERSON AGAIN."

But the most surprising thing I learned?

Brands desperately needed help.

I had this assumption they knew everything but quickly realized that when they *don't* know how to do something, it's usually easier to hire an outside party to get them up to speed (vs. the red tape of hiring someone full-time).

So the pitch for my new business became simple: I'll help you accomplish your brand objectives through influencer marketing.

That led to my first $50,000 check.

I would ultimately run that agency for seven years, facilitate 1,000+ campaigns, pay out millions of dollars to creators, and discover countless secrets to unlocking brands' massive budgets.

The best part is these secrets don't just apply to running an agency.

The secrets are universal and can be leveraged by anyone with an audience to transform their life and business.

Yes, even if the only "employee" in your business is...you.

Whether you have a reach of 100 or 100,000,000...

Whether that audience is online or offline...

Whether you create videos, podcasts, social media content, articles, courses, newsletters, or events...

Whether you consider yourself a "creator" or "influencer," or those titles don't resonate with you at all...

If you have *influence* over a body of people...

I will teach you how to become a *Sponsor Magnet* so you can finally earn what you deserve.

But first, let's ensure you're not making nine common mistakes that will prevent you from landing consistent, well-paying deals.

1. Don't aimlessly create; define your *Surprising Transformative Promise*.

Imagine your dream brand stumbles upon one of your videos or hears a clip from your podcast.

Will they be able to instantly envision partnering with you?

If you have even a shred of doubt, that's a problem.

A parenting influencer once asked me, "Why am I not getting any sponsorships from food brands?"

I looked at her page, and there wasn't a single post featuring food. The page was filled with her travels, family pictures, and selfies.

There's nothing wrong with that, but brands ask a singular question when evaluating a prospective partner: will this person's audience be influenced by them when they recommend our brand/product/service?

My advice to that parenting influencer? Start posting quick and easy weeknight meal ideas.

She got a sponsorship from a food brand soon after.

Now imagine that brands are *so busy* they don't have time to watch one of your videos or listen to a clip from your podcasts. Blue sky thinking, I know; everyone finds time for *your* podcast. But let's imagine a crazy world where not *everyone* does.

Instead, when they stumble upon your social media profile bio or the "About" section of your website, you have less than 30 seconds to illustrate that your audience is filled to the brim with their ideal customers.

How are you going to do it?

By defining your **Surprising Transformative Promise or S.T.P.**

- Surprising = Unique
- Transformative = Outcome-focused
- Promise = It's not about you

Olivia, a fashion creator, originally had a social media bio that read:

   "The cutest everyday style & the best sales   Petite outfits"

After coaching her through the S.T.P. process, she decided a better bio would be:

- Surprising = Focused on petite clothing
- Transformative = You'll look and feel your best
- Promise = Helping you (her follower)

Take a pause and reflect on your "identity" (without getting too existential).

Why do people follow you, your work, or your business?

What do they get out of it?

If you don't know, ask them.

When my friend Jay Clouse wondered why people followed him, he posted, "What words or ideas do you associate with me or my work?" and got many deep responses.

If you're still struggling to figure out your S.T.P., here's an easy trick to unblock you.

Add "to" or "so that" to articulate the transformation.

For example, when I did this exercise for my own business, Creator Wizard, I came up with:

"Helping you find and negotiate your dream sponsor-ships so that you stop leaving thousands on the table."

The transformation I'm promising is quite clear, right?

Think back to Olivia's new S.T.P.: "Helping you find petite outfits to look and feel your best."

When a fashion brand that specializes in petite clothing reads that, they'll instantly think, "Everyone in her audience has the problem our product solves."

There's one more hidden benefit to designing a rock-solid S.T.P:

Your audience will grow.

Remember, people don't care about you. Well, OK, maybe that's not 100% true. Your family cares about you. Your friends care about you. And your pets *probably* do too (cats are like 50/50).

But your audience - the people who the brand wants to reach - they don't really care about you.

They care about how you make them feel and what you can help them achieve.

If you're still skeptical, what if I told you Olivia's audience grew 54% larger within just a few months after designing her S.T.P.?

2. Don't pitch random brands; ask your audience.

Many first float into sponsorships because it seems the easiest and most obvious way to fund their creations and monetize their influence.

They usually start by direct messaging or emailing brands they already love:

> *"I've been using your product for three years and it'd be great to collaborate!"*

Not only is that a terrible pitch (we'll get to why in Chapter 1), but it completely ignores the most important thing:

It's not about you.

Brands don't care how much you love them. That's table stakes. Spamming their direct messages with heart emojis won't cut it.

And no, the emoji with the money tongue won't work either (put your phone down).

They care about finding more *customers* (psst: that's your audience).

Even if you have brands pitching *you* regularly, it's a big problem if your only criteria for taking a deal is whether you use their product or service.

This is why partnerships often underperform; just because you think a brand is cool doesn't mean your audience will.

A better approach is to open a proactive dialogue to learn more about them and the types of brands they'd be into.

Here's a simple exercise.

Create the following survey form and send it to your audience:

Hey [name]!

I want to learn more about you! I'm planning my next series of [videos/posts/podcasts/events, etc.], and I want to ensure they serve you. It would mean a lot to me if you took a second to answer a few questions.

- *What type of job do you have?*

- *Do you have a partner?*
- *Do you have kids?*
- *How and when do you typically interact with my [videos/ posts/podcasts/events, etc]?*
  - *Is it in line at the coffee shop for two minutes?*
  - *Or do you sit down every weekend and catch up on my most recent [videos/posts/podcasts, etc.]?*
- *What problems do you have, and what keeps you up at night?*
- *Is there any type of product or service that you wished I offered that I don't, and why?*
- *What types of brands/products/services are you using or interested in right now and why?*
- *Are there other people you'd like to see me collaborate with? Why?*

Thanks!

[Your name]

If you feel intimidated by doing a full-blown survey or think your audience won't be into that, you can ask these questions casually during in-person conversations or one at a time on social media.

One of my students, Christian Taylor, felt constrained by the limited number of brands he could partner with in his online security niche.

However, after surveying his audience he discovered 70% were interested in *home security* as well.

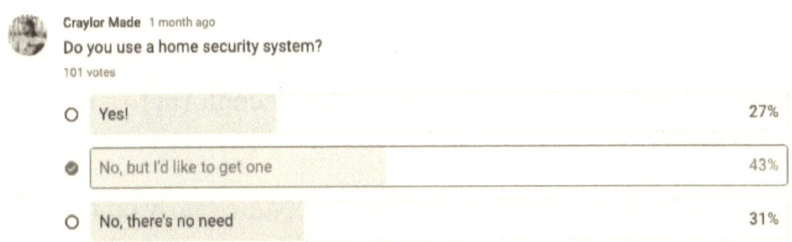

He was shocked and immediately crafted a pitch to a large residential alarm company.

It was instantly clear to him how he could integrate a brand like that into his videos in a way that felt authentic and audience-first.

The goal is to stop operating in an echo chamber and better understand what makes your audience tick.

Armed with robust psychographic data, your pitch shifts from "I love you, please pay me" to "Here's proof that a bunch of people in my audience want to hear about your brand."

3. Don't target giant brands; be realistic.

It's a shame how pervasive the myth is that you need a minimum audience size to work with sponsors.

Perhaps a brand even told you once, "We only work with people who have X,000 followers" or "Your reach needs to be Y,000," so you just assumed that's every brand's policy.

Nope.

I've helped hundreds of people with modest reach land four- and five-figure sponsorships.

However, the deals they usually land do not conform to a typical "brand deal."

It's a mistake to reach out to gigantic companies early on in your journey and say, *"Hey, I love your brand! Let me spread the word about it."*

The brand will likely take one look at your platform and see that you're getting an average of 300 views per video.

Do you think that's going to move the needle for them?

Unlikely.

Instead, it's far more effective to research a smaller- or medium-sized brand's social media presence, identify gaps or opportunities in their strategy, and message them proposing a different approach.

> *"I have some ideas for how you could tell your brand story in a more compelling way. For example, instead of only posting 1x a week on your brand's social media, I can create 12 videos a month that you post directly on your handles to increase that cadence to 4x a week. Take a look at my platform, which serves as my portfolio."*

Did you feel that shift?

That was the brand sitting up a little straighter in their chairs.

Maybe you sat up straighter, too?

Now, let's say the size of your audience begins to grow.

Instead of hundreds of views per video, you're getting thousands.

What you propose to a brand now combines consulting, content creation for the brand's use, and, yes, natively posting on your platform.

The brand just sat up straighter still!

Time to fast-forward and imagine you've now achieved serious scale.

You're getting tens or hundreds of thousands of views.

Creating and posting the content natively on your platform becomes the singular thrust of your proposal.

The brand is now sitting up *so* straight they've risen out of their chair and are walking over to personally hand you a gigantic bag of cash with a money symbol on it.

Sponsorship Continuum

Create content for brand to use on its O&O, third-party, or ads. Consulting. Your platform = your portfolio — Combo of consulting, content for brand use, and you post natively on your platforms — Create & post natively on your platforms

What you pitch as your **experience, audience,** and **influence** grow

Regardless of how far along you are on your journey, you can use this Sponsorship Continuum to know who and what to pitch.

4. Don't envy others' deals; pitch that brand next.

One gripe I hear often is, "How come *that* person landed a sponsorship with my dream brand? I've never seen them talk about it, and *I've* used it for years."

Instead of spiraling, there's a simple way to turn this into a sponsorship opportunity for *you*.

If a brand decides to partner up with another person in your industry, two things are true:

1. Brands are now investing money into your niche/content format
2. Brands rarely partner with just a single person

The first thing a brand usually does after it completes a successful sponsorship with one person is think, "Who else can we partner with?"

Spoiler alert: that's you!

It's now your chance to reach out to that brand and say:

> *[Hey name],*
>
> *I saw that fantastic partnership you're doing with [other person]. Are you looking to amplify this campaign further?*

My audience is primed for your product. That amazing feature [other person] talked about is the exact thing my audience has said they're looking for.

I also noticed you're using paid media to boost your content for this campaign. I can create additional assets you can use across your social platforms.

Are you free on Thursday at 10 am to chat about this?

Thanks,

[Your name]

Remember, this is *not* a zero-sum game.

By the way, you don't have to wait for someone else to get sponsored to get the attention of your dream brand.

All it takes is simply getting on their radar so they know you exist.

Do you think brands have time to keep tabs on every single *potentially* influential customer?

Especially if you've never publicly stated your love for the brand?

The best way to command their attention is to start shouting them from the rooftops!

Tag them on social media. Include a shout-out in your next newsletter, then email them the blurb.

The more you become a "known quantity," the quicker you'll be remembered when the brand recruits for its next campaign.

"But Justin, why would they pay me if I talk about them for free?"

When brands have specific marketing objectives, there are almost always talking points they need you to hit or sound bites they need you to say.

Things you'd never do or say on your own in a simple shout-out.

Don't overthink this.

The closer you get to the brand, the closer you'll be to landing a sponsorship.

5. Don't work with toxic brands; find ones that respect you.

The quickest way to convince yourself that sponsorships suck is to stay attached to toxic brand relationships indefinitely.

"The money's OK," you think. "It'll get better. They'll get nicer."

It never does, and they never do.

I mean, sure, the brand gives you crippling anxiety 24/7, but at least you're getting $100 and a free bag of potato chips every few months!

The only way to permanently sever that toxic tether is to stop running from fear.

Firing a brand is not fun. They might get mad. They might try to blame you.

But the longer you refrain from doing what needs to be done, the less mental space you can devote to building healthier partnerships with brands who respect you.

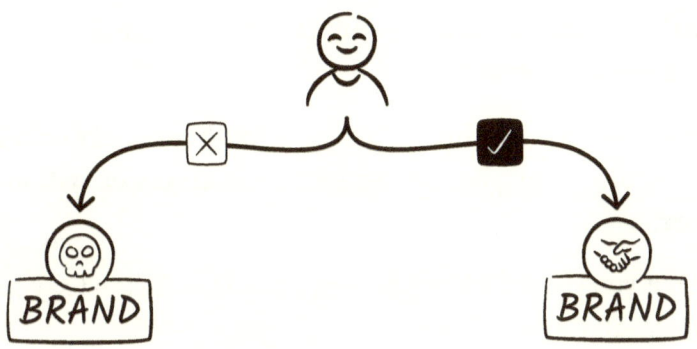

Still trying to figure out what to say to end a partnership?

Hey [name],

I've enjoyed working with you over the last X months and am so proud of our work together.

Moving forward, I've decided to focus on other projects and will no longer be able to continue our partnership.

I wish you all the best.

[Your name]

Then hit send.

Congrats, you're free.

6. Don't let your ego control you; be objective.

Think back to the last time a brand got you heated.

Maybe they lowballed you during the negotiation.

Maybe they're asking for more stuff even though the deal you signed doesn't cover that.

Maybe you've been waiting for feedback for three weeks only for them to finally email you and ask for a revised version within 24 hours!

Please put your pitchfork down. Hey, I saw that. I didn't say half-way down. All the way down.

Remaining calm and composed in these moments will differentiate you from every other hot-headed partner.

The reality is that a sponsorship is a business transaction.

The brand is paying you money to accomplish an objective.

Of course, you need to safeguard your integrity and relationship with your audience, but don't lose sight of why the brand hired you.

If you feel strongly that the brand is wrong, simply explain why their request will take them further from their objectives.

And don't worry, we'll cover exactly what to do when brands lowball you (Chapter 2), try to add more work (Chapter 5), or ask for unreasonable changes (Chapter 6).

Just don't be a pain in the butt when you reply to the brand. Your wallet will thank you.

7. Don't bad-mouth brands; be diplomatic.

There's an insidious narrative spreading that every brand is evil and trying to take advantage of unsuspecting creators. "I'm fighting back!" the social media tirades proclaim, naming and shaming the brands publicly.

And it might work...the first time.

That overdue invoice will finally get paid or the brand will apologize for only offering "free product" as compensation.

But *new* brands will see those posts and decide partnering with them just isn't worth the risk. Any time issues arise or there are new campaign requirements, will that creator scurry to social media to drag the brand? Not a good look.

Now, it's one thing to hold brands accountable for legitimate fraud, but the grievances most creators share publicly are not that.

Snags are part of running a business so learning to be professional and diplomatic will take you very, very far.

8. Don't ignore the changing world around you; plan for the future.

When short-form video content started growing in popularity, I crossed my arms like a curmudgeon and looked down my nose. "I'm a YouTuber. I'm not going to do *that*."

So I watched from the sidelines for years as others grew massive audiences by embracing a new format.

When I finally broke down and decided I couldn't ignore short-form's popularity any longer, I felt regret.

Not because my peers had surpassed me.

But because I had refused to believe the world was changing around me.

There were two main reasons I reversed my stance:

1. My audience started spending more and more time learning via short-form
2. Brands started shifting sponsorship dollars over to short-form

If you're ever wondering whether you should pay attention to a hip new platform or format, use that two-part litmus test to decide what to do.

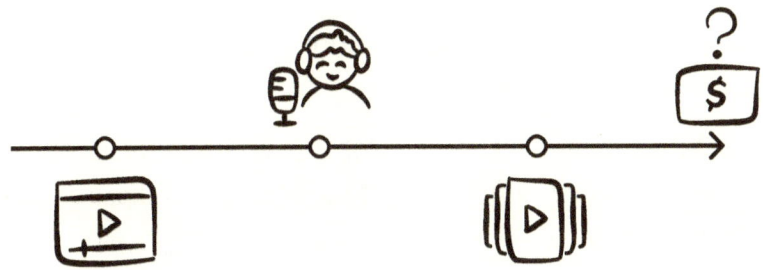

Don't be like me and put your head in the sand (protip: it always leads to a swift kick in the rear).

You must keep your eye on the horizon and anticipate where the world is going, not where it is right now.

9. Don't outsource the "business stuff" to a manager, agent, or broker; learn it yourself.

One of the most common questions I get from those who want more sponsorships is:

"Can I hire someone to do this for me and just give them a cut? I'm too busy to do this myself."

Here are the four reasons why you should not hire representation like a manager, agent, or broker:

1. The financial incentives are misaligned

If the only way your rep eats is if they get a 20% cut of your sponsorships, there will almost certainly be deals they'll tell you to take that may not be in your best interest.

2. You're growing their contact list, not yours.

Imagine you hire a rep and start getting some sponsorships. Awesome!

But you're creative so you don't want to handle any "business stuff," and you *especially* don't want to be CCed on those emails (that's why you hired the rep, right?).

You do a few sponsorships. You get paid. All is well.

But then you get into a tricky situation with your rep where you disagree.

They want you to take a sponsorship you don't think is a good fit. They get mad. You're annoyed, but you brush it off.

Then, over the next few weeks and months, you start hearing from your rep less and less.

They start sending you fewer deals. You still get some occasionally, but there's a noticeable decline.

You start getting even more annoyed.

You tell your rep they're not pulling their weight.

They get even angrier and tell you,

   "Maybe we shouldn't work together anymore."

"FINE!" you say...

"FINE!" they say back.

And then there you are, "rep-less" with no connections to those ten brands you worked with over the last year.

Not ideal.

3. You don't know how you're being represented in the market.

When I ran my influencer marketing agency, I worked with managers, agents, and brokers quite a bit, and the reality is that some have a bizarre "gatekeeper" complex.

When we needed time-sensitive revisions or insights from the people they represented, it would sometimes take *days* to get a response.

I've even had reps cuss me out!

By the way, what happens in those scenarios?

Do you think brands want to work with those reps' creators anymore?

The creators may be charming people, but because their reps are nightmares, that creator gets put on a "DO NOT HIRE" list.

These lists exist (I've seen them).

You want to avoid finding yourself on one of them.

Sadly, many creators have no idea their reps are insane.

I've even been tempted to reach out to several creators and say, *"Do you know how your rep is making you look? They're causing you to lose business."*

My rule of thumb: Preserve your reputation by forgoing representation.

4. You're robbing yourself of an education.

If you want to make more money from sponsorships, your #1 priority should be understanding how the advertising puzzle pieces fit together in your niche or industry (genius move buying this book by the way. It'll help a lot).

When you start interacting with brands & partners, it's critical you learn what things they find most valuable about you.

In my experience, when you work with a rep, their priority is deal volume, which often means you become just another commoditized "talent" on their roster.

But when *you* have a direct connection with your brand partners, you'll start to realize there are many things you can do for them that may not conform to a standard sponsorship.

Maybe it's helping them think through their social media strategy.

Maybe you can connect them with your friends who would also be a great fit for a partnership.

Maybe it's offering a value-add post that wasn't required in the contract.

It's paramount to get an "in-the-trenches" education about how your business model will work and be sustainable.

BECOMING A SPONSOR MAGNET

Let me drill this into your head one more time.

If you're still thinking:

"I just want to focus on the creative stuff and let someone else handle all the other business details..."

Then this will always be just a hobby for you.

On the other hand, if you want to have a long-term career, it's time to take true ownership of this incredible asset you're creating.

To recap, here are the nine most common mistakes that will prevent you from landing consistent, well-paying sponsorships (and what to do instead):

1. Don't aimlessly create; define your Surprising Transformative Promise.

2. Don't pitch random brands; ask your audience.

3. Don't target giant brands; be realistic.

4. Don't envy others' deals; pitch that brand next.

5. Don't work with toxic brands; find ones that respect you.

6. Don't let your ego control you; be objective.

7. Don't bad-mouth brands; be diplomatic.

8. Don't ignore the changing world around you; plan for the future.

9. Don't outsource the "business stuff" to a manager, agent, or broker; learn it yourself.

So, here's the deal. There are actually ten mistakes but I saved the worst for...well, the bottom.

10. Don't pull a sponsorship strategy out of your butt; create a system.

Use my 8-step Sponsorship Wheel system to land consistent, well-paying partnerships.

The Sponsorship Wheel is a sales pipeline.

The concept of a sales pipeline might sound intimidating if you've never had a corporate job, but it's basically a way for businesses to track how close a prospect is to becoming a paying customer.

And most creators oversimplify what it takes to close a deal successfully.

This is how most think it works:

- A sponsorship opportunity pops into their inbox
- They negotiate on the price and the brand either says yes or no
- If yes, they produce the deliverables, then publish

But what *actually* happens in real life?

You get a rude awakening after sending drafts to the brand.

Instead of approving the drafts immediately, the brand returns with *feedback*.

"Hey, can you redo this?" they say.

And you think, "Wait a minute, I think this is good. I don't get it?"

But the brand says, "Unless you update this, we can't move forward, and we won't pay you."

So you get smart next time.

"I'm going to add language to the contract that says what type of feedback would constitute a redo."

This way, the brand can't give you an arbitrary reason to rewrite your post or reshoot a video (like they disliked the color of your shirt).

Or maybe the brand gives you an initial round of feedback, you make the changes, and then they come back with *something else*.

"Ugh, fine," you think.

You revise it, and then there's *another* round of requests.

Before you know it, you're seven rounds deep with no end in sight.

So you add language in your agreements that protects you from those scenarios.

But then the next company comes back and says, "We just don't like what you created. It's not what we had in mind."

What do you do?

Do you fight them on it?

Do you make an argument for why it's going to perform well?

That's a tricky conversation.

You know what would've been better?

Getting their buy-in ahead of time by sharing a concept of how you'll bring the partnership to life!

Some companies *will* ask you for this, but a lot won't, so it's your job to send them a concept to greenlight.

Now we're in business.

You create the deliverables, the brand approves them, and you finally hit publish or complete the activation.

You submit your invoice, all the annoying vendor paperwork and tax forms, and screenshots of how your work performed.

Then, a few weeks or months later, the money hits your bank account.

Woohoo! You're a Sponsor Magnet.

But wait, *are you?*

Why isn't the brand reaching out to work with you again? Instead, you're back at square one, hustling to convince a *new* brand to hire you.

The final missing step is submitting a "Post-Campaign Report" with quantitative *and* qualitative analyses that, critically, help the brand understand that you've uncovered *new* opportunities for them.

> *"But Justin, the brand didn't ask for that. They seemed fine with screenshots of my metrics."*

The truth is that brands often don't look beyond the numbers.

It's *your job* to provide deeper context that the numbers simply won't explain.

Because let's face it: not every sponsorship will do well.

A lot will perform *average.*

Some will downright fail.

Those are the scariest ones. It's terrifying to ask a brand, "How'd it go?"

"Thanks for asking. It actually sucked." Yikes.

Now, a brand will rarely say that to your face (more on why in Chapter 8), but the key is realizing that your analysis serves as the mechanism to pitch them on the *next* campaign.

Speaking of pitching, remember we jumped right into the negotiation at the beginning because the company reached out to *us*?

Did you consider that the company also contacted 20 other people simultaneously?

If you knew that was happening, would you have changed your approach?

Sure, you got *this* deal, but what about those times when you lost a deal?

Maybe you didn't correctly pitch the brand on why you were the best person for the job (amongst the 20 others they were vetting).

Let's set the record straight.

A pitch is not just when you contact a brand cold through their DMs or press email.

A pitch is not just reserved for creators at the beginning of their journeys.

Understanding how to properly craft a sponsorship pitch, whether inbound or outbound, will help brands understand why they should pay you 2x or 3x the amount others might be charging.

A pitch is also something else.

It's the grease that keeps your Sponsorship Wheel spinning.

Put another way: Every sponsorship should start AND end with a pitch.

When you submit your analysis to the brand in Step 8, *you return to Step 1 and pitch them on the next collaboration.*

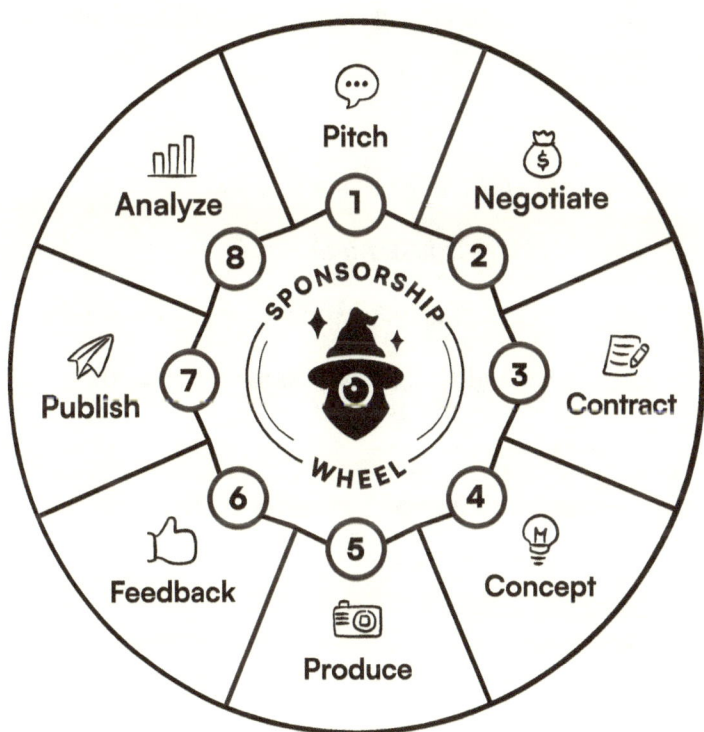

There you have it.

My Sponsorship Wheel framework:
- Step 1: Pitch
- Step 2: Negotiate
- Step 3: Contract

- Step 4: Concept
- Step 5: Produce
- Step 6: Feedback
- Step 7: Publish
- Step 8: Analyze

We've now reached an important moment. You've given me the benefit of the doubt thus far but I know I'm still battling that skeptical voice inside you:

"I'm not an influencer..."

"I don't have a big following on social media..."

"My content/business is just too niche..."

"No brands or companies would ever want to work with me..."

I hear you. I understand you. I *was* you for many years.

But I'm willing to bet...

Even if you're not an 'influencer'...*you **do** influence people.*

Even if you don't have a big following...*those that **do** follow you are extremely engaged.*

Even if your business is niche...*there **are** niche brands you can serve.*

Even if it seems like no brands would ever want to work with you...*have you actually **asked** them?*

Set aside your hesitations and concerns. Suspend your disbelief. Open your mind to a better, more abundant future for yourself and your business.

A future where you build lucrative, longer-term brand partnerships.

A future where you master pitching and pricing so you stop leaving thousands on the table.

A future where you unearth the confident negotiator inside of you.

Can you guess the step-by-step system that will make that future a reality?

The Sponsorship Wheel.

Bonus:

I've turned my Sponsorship Wheel into a sweet template to help you take action over the following chapters. My Sponsorship Wheel Tracker will help you:

- Track your pitches to brands and companies
- Remember when to follow up (with built-in formulas)
- Manage your partnerships once you land the deals

Download it for free here: ***sponsormagnet.com/tracker***

Pitch

To understand why consistent outbound pitching is so important, we can learn from one of nature's most cunning strategists: the honey bee.

In a hive, the "Scout" bees venture into the surrounding landscape to determine the best places to forage. They then return and communicate their findings with an incredible "dance" (that would probably go viral).

Does the entire colony promptly fly to that spot to exploit the location? Not quite.

About 20% of the Scout bees do something *different*.

They ignore their peers and choose to explore the unknown.

Most times, they fly around and find nothing.

But *sometimes,* they discover a new location far superior to the original that will ensure the colony's continued survival.

This phenomenon, called the **Exploit-Explore Tradeoff,** can be found not just in nature but in many aspects of our personal and professional lives.

Choosing a familiar restaurant over a new one? You're exploiting.

Searching for a new job over your current one? You're exploring.

This is why relying solely on inbound leads from brands is a trap.

When everything's going great (audience growth, macroeconomic stability, etc.), creators mistakenly think they can *exploit* the short-term deal flow, which will last forever.

The other problem with inbound opportunities is the campaigns are almost always "fully-baked."

This means things like:
- Budget
- Activation strategy
- Scope of work/deliverables
- Terms
- Timeline
- Number of partners

...are locked in.

While it's true these deals will be "easier" to close, it also means that your ability to influence the partnership dynamics (i.e., how much they pay you) is minimal.

This is why devoting ongoing chunks of your time to *exploring* outbound opportunities is critical.

The reality is most of your pitches will be dead-ends.

You'll have many conversations and video calls with brands where you think it's leading somewhere promising, only for them to say, *"It's just not the right time."*

But eventually, a handful of those discussions will bear fruit.

Fruit so ripe and delicious that eating anything else will become unappetizing.

Critically, fruit bore from *exploration* will ensure the continued survival of your business.

But you don't want to simply *survive,* right?

You want to be a Sponsor Magnet that *thrives.*

And to thrive you must learn how to craft a sponsorship pitch that no brand will ignore.

Common mistakes and pitfalls when pitching.

- Making your pitch too "you" focused
- Direct-messaging the brand on social media
- Emailing the wrong person

In 2009, when I was still working in the medical device industry, I didn't know what a "pitch" was.

What I *did* know was that April and I were planning our honeymoon, and I was desperate to get some travel discounts in exchange for promotion on our social media accounts.

April was pretty skeptical but (bless her heart) said, "Knock yourself out."

Picture this: It's my lunch break. I'm hunkered down in my little cubicle. Earbuds in, office chatter tuned out. Probably listening to metal.

I've got a self-satisfied smirk on my face as I draft this pitch:

Subject line: Marketing/Business Opportunity for The Paradise Koh Yao Resort

Hello,

My name is Justin Moore, and my fiancée, April, has a YouTube channel with over 2,000,000 total views and over 29,000 subscribers (youtube.com/aprilathena7). We will be getting married in August and going on our honeymoon to the Phuket area shortly thereafter. We would love to stay at The Paradise Koh Yao Resort as we have heard many good things about the hotel on TripAdvisor. We would like to stay in the Hilltop Pool Villa from August 15-19, 2011. We were wondering if you might be interested in discussing a possible business opportunity. In return for complimentary or discounted room rates at your hotel, we will do a "sponsored" video on April's YouTube channel and will talk about the wonderful amenities of The Paradise Koh Yao Resort and also feature video footage of the hotel (with permission).

We believe it would be a great opportunity for The Paradise Koh Yao Resort to promote the excellent services and room options it has to offer and also gain exposure in the social media community (YouTube, Facebook, Twitter, etc.). It would be much appreciated if you could pass along this message to the appropriate individual at your hotel (perhaps anyone in the Marketing, Public Relations or Customer Outreach departments).

Thank you for your kind consideration!

Sincerely,

Justin and April

"It's not so bad," you're thinking.

I appreciate the pat on the head, but it's terrible for a few reasons:

1. I didn't even bother to look up the name of the person I was emailing. Just hit them with the classic, "Hello." It's not like first impressions count or anything, right?

2. The first three sentences were all about me, me, me. The company doesn't know who I am and probably doesn't care about our social media reach!

3. I asked for complementary OR discounted rooms in the same breath. Great job negotiating against yourself before they even replied, genius.

Worst yet, I decided, *"Gee, that was enough hard work for one day..."* and proceeded to copy and paste this exact pitch to hundreds of hotels in Asia, simply swapping out the name in the subject line and body.

Marketing/Business Opportunity for the Sheraton Hong Kong Hotel & Towers - a possible business opportunity. In return for c

Marketing/Business Opportunity for the Marco Polo Hong Kong Hotel - a possible business opportunity. In return for complim

Marketing/Business Opportunity for the Luxe Manor - a possible business opportunity. In return for complimentary or discoun

Marketing/Business Opportunity for the Harbour Grand Kowloon - a possible business opportunity. In return for complimentar

Marketing/Business Opportunity for the Hyatt Regency Hong Kong Tsim Sha Tsui - a possible business opportunity. In return f

Marketing/Business Opportunity for the Dorsett Regency Hotel Hong Kong - a possible business opportunity. In return for con

Marketing/Business Opportunity for the Novotel Citygate Hong Kong - a possible business opportunity. In return for complime

Marketing/Business Opportunity for the Mira Hong Kong - a possible business opportunity. In return for complimentary or disc

Marketing/Business Opportunity for the Grand Hyatt Hong Kong - a possible business opportunity. In return for complimentar

Marketing/Business Opportunity for the L'Hotel Nina et Convention Center - a possible business opportunity. In return for com

Marketing/Business Opportunity for the Lanson Place Hotel - a possible business opportunity. In return for complimentary or

Marketing/Business Opportunity for the W Hong Kong - a possible business opportunity. In return for complimentary or discou

I sense that you're face-palming but you're going to feel so silly when I tell you all the awesome replies I started getting:

"Undeliverable."

"Please remove my email address from your list."

"Thanks, but no thanks."

OK...the replies weren't ideal.

I quickly learned there are two critical components of every successful pitch:

- What you say
- Who you send it to

If you screw either of those up, your chances of getting ghosted or rejected skyrocket.

And you'll probably convince yourself that pitching doesn't work (it does).

Make your pitch about them, not you.

One of the most common messages I receive is:

"My videos/podcast/posts/events are killin' it right now! I get XYZ,000 views/downloads/impressions/attendees every month. Can you help find brands to sponsor me?"

Now, on the surface, this is a reasonable question. However, there's a critical flaw with the framing of this mindset:

It's not about you (sorry).

Firstly, when you reach out to brands, your pitch has to focus on them rather than you.

I know how stoked you might feel that your latest podcast episode got five times the usual downloads, but the brand doesn't care. They don't know who you are.

OOPS. They just deleted your email.

Your #1 priority must be articulating how to help the brand achieve specific business outcomes. Outcomes that are rarely as simple as "get more views."

"Wait, hold up, Justin! Won't brands be excited about getting tons of eyes and ears on their products/services? My audience is a perfect fit for their brand!"

Not really. Again, they don't know you. And there are lots of people on the Internet with large audiences/reach. *Delete.*

Remember, even if you're trying to pitch them something you feel is "low-risk," they don't have heaping piles of cash lying around to pay random people who reach out.

There's another huge problem here: it's terrible for you, too.

If you somehow land a deal, you're now trapped with a sub-optimal rate precedent and it will be extremely difficult to negotiate your way out of that hole down the line.

What happens when you start doing even better than you are now?

One of the most significant opportunities for creators I coach is helping them detach their rates from their views/downloads/impressions/audience size.

This is often a giant barrier to landing lucrative sponsorships, especially for smaller creators.

A critical mindset shift is realizing that while brands don't have piles of cash lying around to sponsor your viral content, they *do* have piles of cash already allocated for their internal initiatives.

So *your* job is to research and identify those initiatives by:
- Analyzing the content they're posting or campaigns they're running
- Reading their press releases & interpreting their marketing strategy
- Sleuthing through their job boards to see what they need help with
- Asking them directly

Once you have the brand's objectives, you can submit a comprehensive proposal illustrating how sponsoring you and your business will help them achieve those desired results.

Want to know what will happen next?

Your contact will then forward that along to their colleagues/ boss (or client, if it's an agency), have a pow-wow, and then collectively decide,

> *"Let's just slide $20,000 of our marketing budget over to this person because it seems like they'll get us closer to our goals."*

Now that you've put your ego in check, let's break down the four key elements of a compelling pitch.

Use the R.O.P.E. Method to craft pitches that are relevant, organic, provide proof, and are easy to execute.

The R.O.P.E. Method is a pitching framework I've honed over many years that has helped thousands of creators cut through the noise and finally get on the radar of their dream brands.

- **"R" stands for "Relevant"** – to a campaign the brand is either currently running or has run in the past.
- **"O" stands for "Organic"** – you can tie your pitch back to organic work you've already published that illustrates your audience has an affinity for their brand or product.
- **"P" stands for "Proof"** – you can show how you've helped other brands achieve results.
- **"E" stands for "Easy to Execute"** – when the brand says they're interested.

Let's pretend we're pitching StarKist Tuna.

Of course, you can substitute this with any brand or company in any niche or industry.

Let's try out this pitch:

> *Hi!*
>
> *I love your brand and am curious if you'd like to collaborate.*
>
> *-Justin*

How do you think the brand will react when you send them that email?

ZZZZZZzzzzzzZZZZZZZ.

That was the brand snoring. It might have even given them night terrors.

Let's check the R.O.P.E. Checklist.

Is this relevant to a campaign they're working on?

Nope.

Does this tie back to organic work you've already posted that illustrates your audience's affinity?

Nope.

Have you shown them any proof that you're credible?

Nope.

Easy to Execute?

If the brand responded and said, "Sounds great, let's do it!"

Well, what are you going to do for them? You didn't pitch them anything.

So, instead, why don't we do a little research?

Was their VP of Marketing recently on a podcast discussing their advertising strategy?

Have they put out any press releases talking about an upcoming product launch?

What about their job boards? Are they recruiting for a Partnerships Manager?

Let's scroll back on their social media posts to see what campaigns they were running *last* year.

Wow, interesting!

In the past, StarKist made some posts about Mediterranean Diet Month.

Fascinating.

So here's what *you're* going to do.

You're going to make an organic post about the Mediterranean Diet Month *before you pitch them.*

Then you send them this:

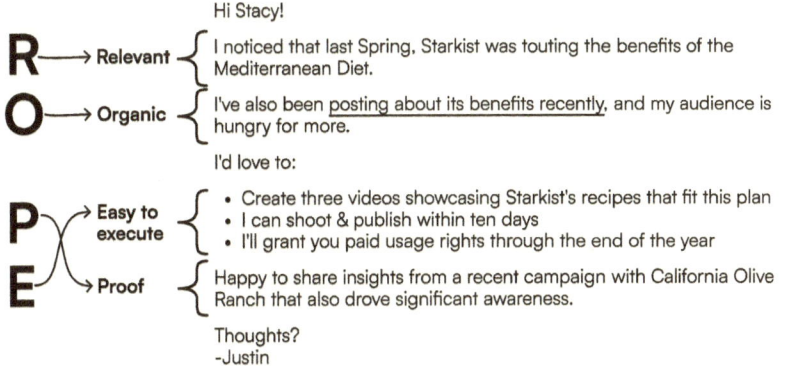

Time to go through the R.O.P.E. Checklist with our revised pitch!

Is this **Relevant** to a campaign they're working on?

Probably!

Most creators think brands reinvent the wheel with their marketing strategies every year but that couldn't be further from the truth.

They typically dust off the same playbook from last year and rerun it.

So, by honing in on a campaign you know they love (they ran it, after all), you will instantly stand out and be **Relevant** to them.

How about **Organic?**

Notice that underlined section in the pitch?

That's where you linked that post you did strategically. The brand can click through, then learn more about your personality and the composition of your audience.

I repeat: You're not linking them to your main social media page.

They won't read your last ten posts or watch 15 of your videos.

They're going to watch 30 seconds of one of them and think, "This person seems like a good fit for our brand!" Or possibly, "I'm immediately reporting this person to the authorities."

Hopefully, not the second one.

The purpose of your **Organic** work is to convince them that your audience already has an affinity for their brand.

How about **Proof?**

You're telling them you just did a deal with another brand in a similar category.

Don't you think they'll want to know how that campaign turned out?

At the very least, to get some non-proprietary, competitive intel?! Almost without question.

What about **Easy to Execute?**

Duh!

Your pitch outlined exactly what you'd do for their brand!

You might think, *"But what if they don't want to do the exact thing I'm pitching?"*

I can almost guarantee you that is what's going to happen.

The brand will say, *"Wow, this is a cool idea. We're not doing that type of campaign right now, but how about this other thing instead? That's a priority for us right now."*

The point is that you gave them something tangible to *react* to.

If you're thinking, *"Justin, this seems like a ridiculous amount of work. I already feel like I'm on a hamster wheel. I don't have time for this!"*

Well, 2009 Justin would've said the same thing!

Because I had to send 100 of those initial crappy pitches to get one or two responses.

Contrast that with Justin of today?

If I spend 15-20 minutes of research max per pitch...

I will receive a response from brands more than 50% of the time.

Remember: Make it about them, not you.

The right (and wrong) way to contact brands so your pitches reach actual decision-makers.

When you send a brand a direct message on social media or email press@brand.com saying, "I love your brand and I've been using your product for five years! Let's collaborate…"

Here's the cold reality:

- The person reading this message is likely handling community engagement, e.g., "Sorry you got a lukewarm burrito; here's a $5 coupon."
- They may not even work at the brand! Social media management might have been delegated to a separate agency.
- They're rarely in charge of paid partnerships
- Worst case: your message got flagged as spam and they never even saw it

Social media DMs, generic email addresses

Specific decision-makers' email addresses

In simpler terms, what do *you* do when you receive a message meant for someone else?

You probably delete it or don't respond.

So, it's a worthwhile exercise to zero in on the exact person who handles partnerships at the brand.

Type this magic search query to uncover the best person to pitch.

To start piecing together the marketing hierarchy at a brand, enter this search query into your favorite search engine:

"[Brand name] [Job title] LinkedIn"

For example, "Nike Influencer Marketing Manager LinkedIn"

I've found search engines to be much better at cataloging employees at your target brands than the search functionality on LinkedIn.

Note: If LinkedIn is not widely utilized in your country, replace it with a more relevant networking platform.

Of course, not all brands have "Influencer Marketing Managers," especially if you're in B2B (Business-to-business) or other niche industries.

Also, not all job titles are made equal.

We've got to be a bit more thoughtful.

Target different job titles depending on the brand's size.

Small brands (less than 15 employees)

When a brand is small, there's probably only one person on its marketing team.

That one marketing person is doing everything:
- Running point on the entire advertising strategy
- Turning off and on social media ads
- Placing ads in local magazines
- Handling partnerships (if they're doing them at all)

Titles to target at small brands:

You can start by looking for a "Director of Marketing," "Marketing Manager," or "Social Media Manager."

Titles to avoid at small brands:

President or anything C-Suite (CEO, COO, CMO)

Mid-size brands (16-100 employees)

As brands grow, it gets trickier.

They begin hiring *multiple* layers of marketing personnel.

I've found it most effective to target the "Manager" level at mid-size brands as they usually have decision-making power but aren't too senior to be entirely removed from the partnership process.

Titles to target at mid-size brands:

Look for "Marketing Manager," "Assistant Marketing Manager," "Influencer Marketing Manager," or anyone with "Partnerships" in their title.

Titles to avoid at mid-size brands:

Anything VP level (e.g., VP of Marketing), President, or anything C-Suite (CEO, COO, CMO)

Big brands (100+ employees)

As brands achieve scale, the name of the game is delegation.

They often have multiple employees handling marketing and may have outsourced things like partnership strategy to an outside advertising agency.

However, always pitch the brand directly first (since they have the ultimate say), and they can refer you to their agency if necessary.

Titles to target at big brands:

Digital Marketing Manager or Coordinator, Influencer Marketing Manager or Coordinator, Influencer Strategist, Partnerships

Manager or Coordinator, Affiliate Marketing Manager or Coordinator, Content Marketing Manager or Coordinator, Creator Partnerships Manager or Coordinator.

Titles to avoid at big brands:

Assistant or Associate Brand Manager, Brand Manager, Social Media Strategist, Social Media Manager, Community Manager, Anything Director-Level (Director of Marketing), Anything VP level (e.g. VP of Marketing), President, Anything C-Suite (CEO, COO, CMO),

If you run into a dead end when pitching a big brand directly, it may be time to reach out to its agency.

When I ran my influencer marketing agency, I paid more than $10,000 to subscribe to services that told you exactly which large advertising agencies were contracted by which big brands.

Eventually, I discovered an easier (and free) way that gets you 95% of the way there.

Search the Internet for "[Brand name] [region] [agency type] agency"

For example, "Nike U.S. PR agency"

You'll almost always be able to find industry news articles about which agency recently "won" the account for that brand.

So, simply insert the job titles below into the magic search query above.

Titles to target at big brands' agencies:

Account Executive, Account Coordinator, Account Manager

Titles to avoid at big brands' agencies:

Account Director, Vice President

Job Title Targeting Matrix

Navigate job titles across brand sizes	Titles to Avoid	Titles to Target
Small Brands (less than 15 employees)	✗ President or anything C-Suite (CEO, COO, CMO)	✓ Director of Marketing ✓ Marketing Manager ✓ Social Media Manager
Mid-Size Brands (16-100 employees)	✗ Anything VP level (e.g., VP of Marketing) ✗ President, or anything C-Suite (CEO, COO, CMO)	✓ Marketing Manager ✓ Assistant Marketing Manager ✓ Influencer Marketing Manager ✓ Anyone with "Partnerships" in their titles
Big Brands (100+ employees)	**Brand** ✗ Assistant or Associate Brand Manager ✗ Brand Manager ✗ Social Media Strategist ✗ Social Media Manager ✗ Community Manager ✗ Anything Director-Level (e.g. Director of Marketing) ✗ Anything VP level (e.g. VP of Marketing) ✗ President ✗ Anything C-Suite (CEO, COO, CMO) **Agency** ✗ Account Director ✗ Vice President	**Brand** ✓ Digital Marketing Manager or Coordinator ✓ Influencer Marketing Manager or Coordinator ✓ Influencer Strategist ✓ Partnerships Manager or Coordinator ✓ Affiliate Marketing Manager or Coordinator ✓ Content Marketing Manager or Coordinator ✓ Creator Partnerships Manager or Coordinator **Agency** ✓ Account Executive ✓ Account Coordinator ✓ Account Manager

But it's not enough to know the types of titles to target.

What if there are multiple people who all look like a good fit?

Which person should you send it to?

Infer the best person to pitch by analyzing job descriptions and social media breadcrumbs.

You can learn a lot from what brands' employees post online.

Here's an excerpt from a real job description of an "Influencer Marketing Manager" at a major consumer brand:

— *Run Content Creator program*

— *Manage micro-influencer campaigns*

— *Oversee video shoots with both influencers and content creators*

— *Work with various influencer agencies to activate new relationships*

What did we just learn from that tiny bit of information?

- This person is likely a decision-maker (they run the program)
- They have a *separate program* to work with smaller partners
- They value video as a content format
- They value partnership marketing so *much* that they're enlisting the help of outside agencies to scale up their efforts

Congrats, you're a grade-A sleuth!

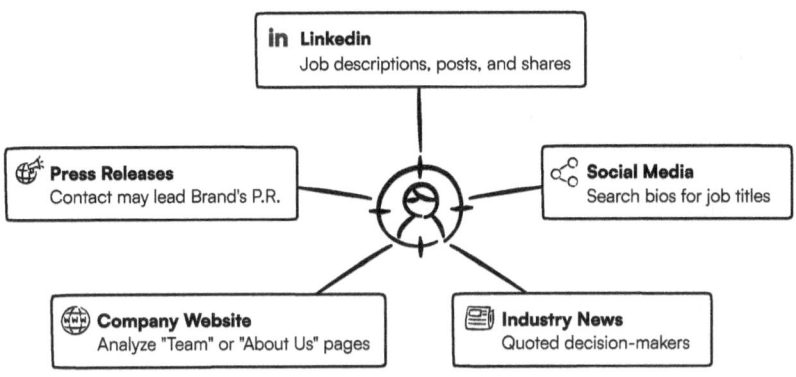

Brand Contact Research Sources

But it's not just job descriptions that are a gold mine.

Maybe this person recently flexed on social media, "So proud that our brand collaborated with XYZ to launch our new ABC campaign! =)"

They always include a smiley face...I don't know why.

From this, we can learn:
- What types of people they're already partnering with
- The audience sizes of their current (or past) partners
- The kinds of initiatives they're currently paying people to promote

So, just remember, all it takes is 15-20 minutes of research to figure out:
- What to say to the brand
- Who to send it to

71

The best way to send a pitch (and not screw it up).

Sending your pitch via email is the best method.

"But Justin..."

Nope. Ssshhhh. Stop.

Email.

Here are my best practices:

- Don't use generic subject lines like "Collaborate?" Instead, lead with whatever was "Relevant" from your R.O.P.E. pitch, e.g., "Idea for #SummerSixPack campaign?"
- In the email body, add your R.O.P.E. pitch and nothing more. Delete any extra fluff or ego-stroking about how awesome you or your audience are. The brand doesn't care.
- Send your pitch on Tuesday, Wednesday, or Thursday. People dig out their inboxes on Monday and mentally check out on Friday.

Perfect Pitch Email Blueprint

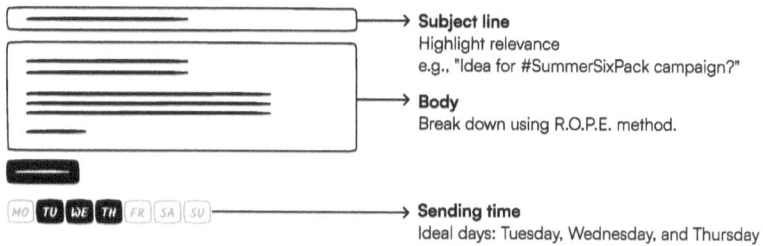

The first time you hit send on a pitch to one of your dream brands, it's a transformative moment.

You're no longer limited to partnering with just the companies that reach out to you.

You're in the driver's seat now.

The world is your oyster, right?

But...uh-oh.

You just refreshed your inbox, and your dream brand...responded.

They said they're interested and want to talk.

What now?

It's time to Negotiate (Step 2).

Bonus:

Claim the free bonuses from this chapter
at *sponsormagnet.com/pitch*

- List of my favorite tools for finding the exact email address of brand contacts
- The R.O.P.E. template for crafting pitches
- The job titles to target depending on the brand's size

Negotiate

A creator booked a coaching call with me because a brand said it had $5,000 left in its quarterly budget and wanted to collaborate.

The problem was that this creator usually charged $10,000 for the requested scope of work (SOW).

At this juncture, most people typically do one of three things:

A. Accept the $5,000 for the full SOW/terms (brand conceding nothing)

B. Say no (politely)

C. Say no (rudely, publicly dragging the brand for lowballing them)

This creator was leaning toward option B.

Instead, I proposed a simple solution:

"Since the brand seems to have budget constraints, why not allow them to pay $5,000 now and the remaining $5,000 next quarter?"

The creator was skeptical that having flexible payment terms would make any difference.

Want to know what the brand said?

> *"You would do that for us?! We didn't even know installments were an option! In that case, can we do a 12-month deal at $5,000 a month?"*

If you can empathize with brands and help them creatively navigate internal red tape, you'll be shocked at how quickly everyone's priorities will align.

Now, I will assume you've had cash flashed in your face before.

While I don't know precisely how much cash, I'm betting one of three things has happened:

- You've tripped over yourself to grab the cash without negotiating
- You've tried asking for more cash but the brand said no or ghosted you
- You've stared blankly at the screen for hours because you haven't the slightest clue whether the cash the brand is offering is totally reasonable or thoroughly insulting

I've been there. Hundreds of creators I've coached have been there.

But even if you've screwed up negotiations in the past, a few simple tweaks to your strategy can change your future.

Common mistakes and pitfalls when negotiating.

- Having "standard pricing" that you send to every brand
- Charging the same as your friends or peers
- Not tying the brand's goals to each package in your proposal

Have you ever had a brand ask you to send over your "media kit" or "rate card" for what you "typically charge for partnerships?"

Don't do it.

If you have a page with rates in your media kit or a page on your site where you allow brands to "book an ad slot" in your podcast or newsletter without even talking to you first...

I want you to drag those pages into the trash can right now.

For extra catharsis, print your media kit out, douse it in lighter fluid, set it ablaze, and maniacally dance around it.

This will symbolize a new beginning for you.

You'll no longer price yourself in a vacuum based solely on your audience size, views, downloads, or any other arbitrary vanity metric.

Why?

Imagine for a moment that you go to the doctor.

You get ushered into a little room and twiddle your thumbs until they arrive.

The doctor opens the door, sits down, and smiles.

You open your mouth to start telling them about your symptoms...

"Sssssh," they say, winking.

The doctor pulls out their little pad, and before learning anything about what problems you're experiencing...

Writes you a random prescription.

They hand it to you, open the door, and leave.

What just happened?!

This is precisely what you do when you provide "standard pricing" to a brand without first asking about their challenges.

Why should you care about the brand's challenges and objectives?

Because, depending on the brand's objectives, *your pricing has to change.*

Use the A.R.C. framework to learn the brand's objectives (Awareness, Repurposing, or Conversion).

There are only three goals that brands care about when forging partnerships:

Awareness, Repurposing, or Conversion, aka my A.R.C. Framework.

100% of the time it will be one, two, or all three of those.

It will never be anything else (don't overthink it).

Awareness campaigns

When you ask a brand, "What would success look like?" and they say things like:

- *"We want to spread the word about our new product launch"*
- *"We're launching in the U.S. after only being available in the U.K."*
- *"We want everyone to know about this cool new feature."*
- *"When people think of XYZ, we want them to associate that with our brand instantly."*

They're clearly after increased **Awareness.**

The KPIs (Key Performance Indicators) that will matter are top-of-funnel metrics like impressions, engagement, or views.

Repurposing campaigns

When a brand says things like:
- *"Can we repost it on social media after you publish it?"*
- *"Can we embed this on our website?"*
- *"Can we run paid advertising with this?"*
- *"Can we put this photo in a magazine ad or plaster it on our trade show booth?"*

That's a **Repurposing** campaign.

The KPIs the brand will want to measure are things like the quality/quantity of assets you can create for them.

Conversion campaigns

When you ask a brand, "What would a 'win' look like?" and they say:
- *"Sales"*
- *"Clicks"*
- *"App Downloads"*
- *"Free trial sign-ups"*

That's a **Conversion** campaign.

The only KPIs they care about are at the bottom of the "funnel." It's got to be trackable, measurable, and attributable.

> *"That's great, Justin. But how does that help me to negotiate more money?"*

Understanding the brand's objectives is critical because their *price sensitivity is different for each type of campaign.*

Campaign Goals – A.R.C. Framework

Campaign Type	KPI (Key Performance Indicator)	Brand's Price Sensitivity
Awareness	PR or Vanity Metrics like Impressions, Engagement, Views	Low (easy to negotiate)
Repurposing	# Assets, Quality, Platform-Specific Cuts, Shiny Objects	Medium (kinda willing to negotiate)
Conversion	Sales, Clicks, CTR (Click-Through Rate), App Downloads	High (hardest to negotiate)

At first glance, this chart may not make sense.

Shouldn't you be able to charge *more* money for a conversion-focused campaign than an awareness-focused one? Since you're driving, you know, actual sales?!

It seems counterintuitive, but let me work backward to explain why it's the opposite.

Conversion campaigns: Understanding brands' secret math

When a brand or agency tells you it's primarily interested in conversions, your contact likely has a specific CPA (Cost Per Acquisition) their boss or client is mandating they hit.

They're thinking,

> *"If we hire this person and they get 10,000 views on their video, based on experience, we're assuming about 10% of viewers will click our sponsored link in the description.*
>
> *Of those 1,000 people, we anticipate 25% (250) will sign up for the free trial.*
>
> *Of those 250 people, we expect 20% (50) to convert to paying customers.*
>
> *Since our product costs $10 per month and the average user subscribes for ten months, our LTV (Lifetime Value) per customer is $100.*
>
> *So, we hope to generate $5,000 in revenue from this partnership (50 paying customers * $100 LTV)."*

Before jumping for joy and imagining how you'll spend the money, remember that the brand doesn't simply want to break even.

They want to turn a *profit* (that's the whole reason to do influencer marketing).

So the amount they'll want to pay you will be a fraction of $5,000.

Whether it's half, a third, or a fourth (or less) depends on each specific brand's target ROI (Return on Investment) and overall risk tolerance.

This is why brands with a conversion-focused goal are often the hardest to negotiate with (i.e., they have the highest price sensitivity).

Rather than getting mad and flaming the brand publicly for lowballing you, you can now empathize with what's happening behind the scenes.

At this point, it's your choice whether to continue negotiating or simply walk away.

Repurposing campaigns: What the brand is thinking (but not saying)

Your negotiating leverage is higher when a brand needs new creative assets to run paid advertising.

Imagine for a moment you're a niche creator with 10,000 followers on a short-form platform. Think about everything you bring to the table.

You're the creative team.

You're the camera crew.

You edit the content.

You market the content.

And, by the way, you can organically distribute the content.

If the brand doesn't hire you, they have to go out there and hire a production company!

And actors and actresses to star in the content.

And someone to edit the content.

And then, when that content is finished, they have to pay all the social media platforms to *run the dang ad* and get it in front of people!

The brand knows this.

And now you know it, too.

So, negotiate harder on these types of deals.

Awareness campaigns: "Squishy" metrics = payday for you

When your brand contact's boss is not constantly barking, "How many sales did that creator we hired drive?!", there's much less scrutiny on the profitability of each specific deal they sign with partners.

Of course, they care from a high level, but the questions the executive team is asking during the quarterly marketing review are things like:

> *"Did we get a lot of eyeballs on our campaign?"*

> *"Did we spread the word?"*

> *"Do people seem excited?"*

Your negotiating leverage skyrockets when the success metrics are "squishy." Pretty sweet, right?

Now that we know the brand's objectives, we're halfway there to setting our pricing.

It's time to figure out the other 50%...what *exactly* do they want you to do for them?

Scope the deal using the D.U.E. Rule (Deliverables, Usage Rights, and Exclusivity).

Many brands can be disorganized when it comes to partnerships.

They waffle even when you ask simple questions about the deal.

It's frustrating, I get it (shouldn't they know this stuff already?)

But the truth is that many brands don't know.

This may be their first partnership, so delving into their strategy and tactics might overwhelm them.

That's why it's so critical to understand the expectations from the jump.

D.U.E. RULE:

✅ *Deliverables*

✅ *Usage Rights*

✅ *Exclusivity*

Deliverables: what exactly does the brand want you to do?

Brands often say,

> *"We love what you create and want to collaborate! How about a few monthly posts or videos on all your platforms?"*

Not going to fly.

How many posts do they want, *specifically?*

What *specific* platforms?

If video, integrated (60-90 second shout-out) or dedicated (focused solely on the brand)?

Short-form or long-form?

If podcast, pre-roll, mid-roll, host-read?

If written, dedicated feature or simple shout-out?

If an event, will the brand be integrated deeply into the programming or just have their logo on signage?

You get the idea.

All these formats have different complexities and require different amounts of effort.

Usage Rights: what else does the brand want to do with your work?

As you now know, repurposing your work is often a big reason brands will want to collaborate with you.

But the one thing they *should not* get is unlimited, free reign to do whatever they want with it *forever.*

So, the first thing to establish is whether the brand wants ***organic or paid usage rights.***

If the brand wants to embed your work on their website or repost it on their social media accounts, this would be considered ***organic usage.***

This is the simplest type of deal, although you still need to be mindful of how long the brand wants to do that for (called the *duration* of usage, which we'll touch on shortly).

Things get a little more complicated when the brand asks for ***paid usage.***

This is where the brand wants to use your work specifically for advertising purposes and spend additional dollars (beyond what they're paying you) to amplify the campaign to reach more eyeballs (beyond those in your audience).

There are three main types of paid usage: **licensing, amplification, and "dark" posts.**

Licensing:

When a brand asks for the raw assets you generate during a partnership so they can run advertising *on their platforms or handles.*

Amplification:

When a brand asks for back-end access to your platform or for a unique code, which allows them to *boost your native post on your platform* so it reaches a larger audience. Amplification is sometimes called boosting or allowlisting.

"Dark" Posts:

When a brand asks for back-end access to your platform or a unique code that allows them to run ads through your platform/handle, *the content will not appear when someone clicks your profile or feed.*

By the way, paid usage can extend outside social media ads on the Internet!

Maybe the brand wants to put your work in a magazine.

Slap your work on a billboard or bus bench.

Heck, maybe they want to use your "Name & Likeness" on their product packaging.

If a brand hasn't asked, trust me, they will eventually.

They may even want "perpetual" usage (sometimes called usage in perpetuity), which means *forever.*

Do you think you should let the brand use your work forever?

No, you shouldn't.

When they ask, always limit the *duration of usage.*

Exclusivity: is the brand prohibiting you from working with their competitors?

When brands pay you to feature them, the last thing they want to see is you promoting their competition a week later.

Not only might that threaten the trust you've established with your audience, but the brand will instantly think you're only in this for the money (good luck trying to get them to hire you again).

However, the *category of exclusivity* should be negotiable.

For example, when my wife and I negotiated a sponsorship with a big cheese brand, they asked for exclusivity in "Snacks."

I don't know about you, but "Snacks" feels like a comprehensive category.

If we were to partner with a potato chip brand a few months later, would that *really* cause our audience not to buy the original brand's cheese products?

I beg to disabrie (please laugh).

So, we made that case to the brand and proposed confining the category to "Snacking Cheeses."

"OK, sounds good," they said without hesitation. Nice.

Also, remember that potato chip brand that hypothetically approached us?

Had the cheese brand said *"no"* to our change of category, and had we also not negotiated the **duration of exclusivity**, this new deal would have been fried. Mashed?

The point is that broad & long exclusivity represents a direct opportunity cost for you. Dollars that would have been in your pocket.

Don't be the creator I know who agreed to five years of exclusivity for a *free mattress* (without realizing it).

Argh.

Pivot what you propose based on what you learn from the brand.

All right, we've got the whole picture now.

We know the brand's objectives and the major deal points.

Now we must decide how to help them accomplish those objectives.

And the tricky part?

You may have to tell the brand that their strategy sucks.

OK, you're not going to say it sucks; you have to do it gracefully.

Even if the brand came inbound asking whether you could make a video to post on your platform, if you know that will not help them accomplish the objectives they outlined...

You have to propose a better strategy.

For example, pretend you ask that same brand,

"*What would a win look like for you?*"

and they say...

"*Well, after you post your video, we want to cut the footage down to a thirty-second asset that we can use to run paid advertising.*"

You should immediately be thinking...

"*Sure sounds like a repurposing campaign!*"

So when they ask how much you charge, instead of saying,

"*Here's my rate for one video post,*"

you're going to say...

"Knowing that your primary objective is using my video for paid advertising, I can actually make you five videos I don't even post.

I can vary the hook, the key messages, and the Calls to Action at the end of each video.

You can then try running all of them as ads and see which performs best."

Want to know the beautiful part of this pivot?

How much you charge is *completely detached* from your audience size or viewership.

Pros and cons of four different pricing strategies (Competitive, Cost-plus, Dynamic, Merit-based).

Regardless of how far you are into your journey, one of the hardest things to know is how much to charge.

It's especially hard if you don't have a pricing strategy.

After coaching hundreds of creators, I've observed three distinct phases everyone goes through.

Phase 1: Competitive pricing

When you don't know what you're doing, asking your friends or industry peers how much they charge seems wise.

The problem is: how do you know that what they're charging is right?

What if they set their rates based on what someone else was charging (who was also winging it)?

Paul Jamison from the Green Industry Podcast told me that before we started working together, his formula for figuring out his rates was to take how much his friends were quoting and charge 5% of that (since his audience was 95% smaller).

Not ideal.

But let's discuss the pros and cons of competitive pricing.

Pros:

1. **You'll likely increase your chances of getting the deal.**

   If you ask your friend how much they charged a particular brand and you quote the brand the same amount, as long as you have a similar reach or platform, you'll probably get the deal!

   You already know the brand is comfortable paying that amount.

Cons:

1. **There's now a power imbalance because you're a commodity.**

   The brand looks at every partner similarly since they can interchange you with someone else without much consequence. You have no differentiation.

2. **You're going to leave money on the table.**

   If you, your friend, and your friend's friend are all pricing yourselves in a vacuum, you'll never truly understand the value you're bringing to the brand. You might later discover the brand was willing to pay you 2x, 3x, or maybe even 10x!

3. It will set a lousy price precedent.

Good luck convincing the brand down the line they should pay you more than the "trial" rate you offered in the beginning.

Competitive pricing feels too basic now, agreed?

Phase 2: Cost-plus pricing

As you grow a bit, you get smarter.

Maybe your hustle is that you upcycle old furniture and share all your cool DIY tips on the Internet.

You've done several sponsorships with paint and sandpaper brands which went pretty well, but then you actually do the math.

You factor in all the time searching for the perfect thrifted specimen, buying all the supplies, hours and hours laboring over the project...

Turns out, you made $2.50 an hour. AWESOME!

So the next time a brand shows interest in a partnership, you think, "I want to recoup my material costs AND make at least $100 an hour."

So, you calculate your costs and add an arbitrary premium.

Seem better?

Well, let's talk about pros and cons of cost-plus pricing.

Pros:

1. You'll cover your costs.

You won't go broke anymore, but you won't get rich.

Cons:

1. **There's still a power imbalance.**

   Now you're just a vendor. Same as a catering company.

2. **You're going to leave money on the table.**

   How do you know whether that brand wasn't willing to compensate you 10x to help them get closer to achieving their objectives? Meanwhile, you're satisfied with getting reimbursed for a $5 paintbrush.

3. **You'll set a lousy price precedent.**

   Good luck convincing the brand that you'll ever be anything other than an "expense."

Darn. Cost-plus pricing had us for a second there.

Phase 3: Dynamic pricing

Things are going a lot better now.

Your audience is growing faster. Your deal flow is accelerating.

You're feeling...too busy?

Seems like every brand wants to spend their ad dollars during the Q4 holiday season.

You get a genius idea: "I'll tell brands that my rates are 2X right now."

Supply and demand, baby!

Hold your horses.

Pros:

1. Short-term revenue maximization.

If a brand is desperate to partner during a critical period and the only way to make it happen is to pay you 3x what they did a few months ago, you'll come out ahead.

Cons:

1. Your repeat business is going to decrease.

Brands can no longer expect consistency from you. When a campaign goes well, the first thing they think is, "How can we keep working with this person?" They want to slot you into their future campaign plans.

Imagine you do a Spring campaign through an agency. Your agency contact tells the brand they should hire you again for the Summer campaign because it went so well. Brand says, "Cool." Agency reaches out to you three months later, only to find you've jacked your rates up? Now they've got to return to the brand with egg on their face.

2. It feels arbitrary to brands and leaves a bad taste.

Do you think the brand will slot you into future campaigns? They don't have time to reach back out whenever they're trying to plan something and ask, *"Are your rates still the same?"* Unless you've grown substantially, don't arbitrarily change your rates every month.

"Justin, stop messing with me. What pricing strategy should I use?!"

The moment of truth has arrived, friend.

Phase 4: Merit-based pricing

Your singular focus when negotiating should be to quantify what it would be worth to the brand if you could help them accomplish their objectives.

You'll quickly realize that different brands value wildly different things.

Pros:

1. **Prioritizes the brand's goals.**

   Brand A may be willing to pay you $10,000 for a single video while Brand B might be willing to pay you *$20,000 for the same scope of work.*

2. **Your rate is detached from your influence.**

   It's no longer just about your audience size or vanity metrics because the brand knows you're invested in the campaign outcome.

3. **Working with you is not an "expense."**

   The brand now views you as a "profit center."

4. **Increased repeat business.**

   The brand wouldn't dream of canceling its contract with you because you blow their minds constantly with new ideas and insights.

Cons:

1. **You'll need to pass on partnerships you would've done before.**

   There's nothing wrong with small deals. They can add up. But your goal should be to make mental space to prioritize higher-value relationships. It will be scary saying "no" the first few times. However, "no" will give you the confidence to say "yes" at the correct times.

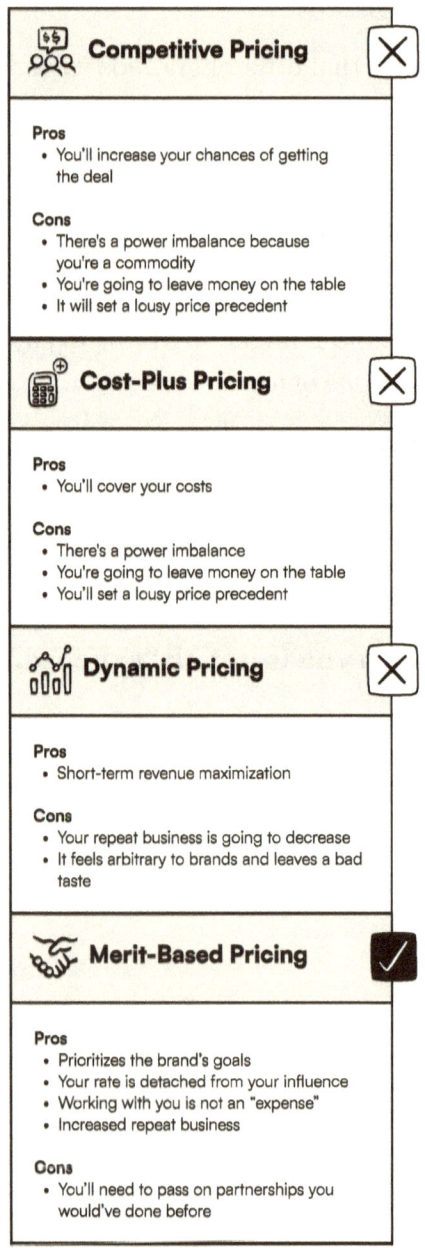

Competitive Pricing ✗

Pros
- You'll increase your chances of getting the deal

Cons
- There's a power imbalance because you're a commodity
- You're going to leave money on the table
- It will set a lousy price precedent

Cost-Plus Pricing ✗

Pros
- You'll cover your costs

Cons
- There's a power imbalance
- You're going to leave money on the table
- You'll set a lousy price precedent

Dynamic Pricing ✗

Pros
- Short-term revenue maximization

Cons
- Your repeat business is going to decrease
- It feels arbitrary to brands and leaves a bad taste

Merit-Based Pricing ✓

Pros
- Prioritizes the brand's goals
- Your rate is detached from your influence
- Working with you is not an "expense"
- Increased repeat business

Cons
- You'll need to pass on partnerships you would've done before

It will be tempting to switch back to non-merit pricing styles to close a deal and get a quick payday. Do so at your peril.

Instead, stick with merit-based pricing so it's clear you and the brand are on the same team, trying to accomplish the same goals.

Now that we've covered pricing *styles*, let's talk about the three main pricing *models*.

Structure the sponsorship using the smartest pricing model (Affiliate, Hybrid, or Flat).

Brands will almost always prefer to pay you on an **affiliate model.**

I mean, why wouldn't they?

If they only have to pay you a 20% commission when you generate a sale, that's their dream scenario.

And even though some affiliate relationships can be lucrative, they often trivialize the work required to generate the content containing the promotion.

Further, haven't you spent years building trust with your audience? Is it fair for you to expend social capital while the brand gets a free endorsement?

No, it's not.

Affiliate marketing:
- Allows brands to commoditize you
- Shouldn't be your primary focus

- Takes a long time to become meaningful
- Can be a fantastic cherry on top of your other revenue streams

Now, it's one thing to stomp your foot on the ground and say, "No more affiliate deals for me!"

It's an entirely different thing for brands to listen.

Many simply won't budge from an affiliate model.

In that scenario, try pivoting to a **hybrid model,** including an upfront base fee *and a back-end kicker.*

Example: A brand offers you a 20% recurring commission on their niche B2B SaaS (Software-as-a-Service). They claim their top affiliates earn $10,000/month.

Let's do some simple math: if their average customer pays $200/month for the software, you'll get a $40 recurring commission from each sign-up. To make $10,000/month, you'll have to generate 250 sign-ups. To generate 250 *paying* sign-ups, you'll likely need to drive 10x the traffic to that brand's offer since only a fraction of your audience will be interested.

Depending on your reach, you might need to do a *ton* of promotion to achieve that. Meanwhile, the brand is happy to have an army of evangelists loudly championing them for free.

I don't know about you, but that seems like a raw deal.

Instead, counter with a hybrid deal of $5,000 upfront (one-time) plus a *10% recurring commission.*

You can explain that as part of the partnership, you will also grant them usage rights to the content you generate for a limited duration to run paid advertising, something their current affiliates almost certainly don't provide.

Even though this represents just over 50% of one month of *potential* affiliate income, you're:

- Receiving guaranteed compensation for your testimonial
- De-risking your time investment
- Making the brand question their current strategy and helping them understand why you're different

When structured well, hybrid deals can make you a ton of money if you have extreme confidence (through psychographic research!) that your audience will go wild for a brand's product or service.

A **flat model**, for many creators, is the holy grail.

Who wouldn't want to receive guaranteed money to do pre-negotiated work without being on the hook for driving any results?

When stated like that, one could argue flat compensation is unfair to the *brand!*

But the reality is many brands prefer this structure because:

- It allows them to set fixed advertising budgets they know they won't exceed
- Their campaign objectives are more awareness-focused vs. conversion-focused
- It requires less internal red tape since it's simple

Flat compensation is also fair for you since:

- Producing content takes time and resources
- Introducing a brand to an immense pool of prospective customers (i.e., your audience) shouldn't be free

- It allows you to focus on creating the best work possible, eliminating income uncertainty.

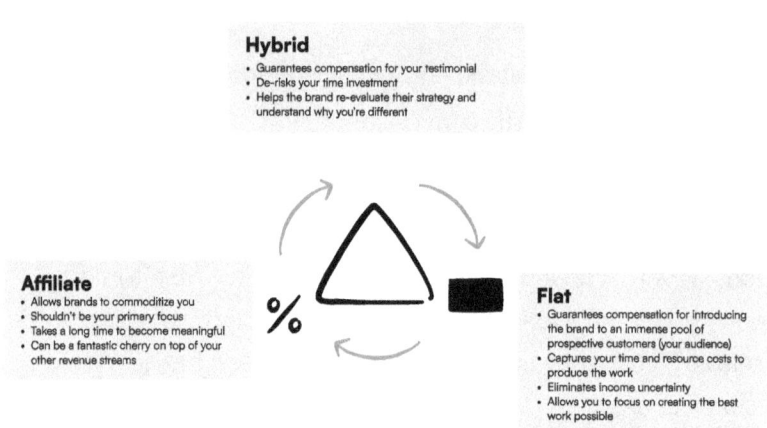

For every partnership, you must ask yourself, "Will affiliate, hybrid, or flat compensation make this deal a win for me *and* the brand?"

Then pick the best model and don't look back.

But wait, shouldn't this deal be a win for someone else as well?

Engineer sponsorships to be "win-win-win".

Most creators aim for win-win collaborations.

The brand wins because you're allowing them to access new prospective customers.

You win because you're getting paid.

Everybody wins, right?

Well, no.

Your audience better be winning, too!

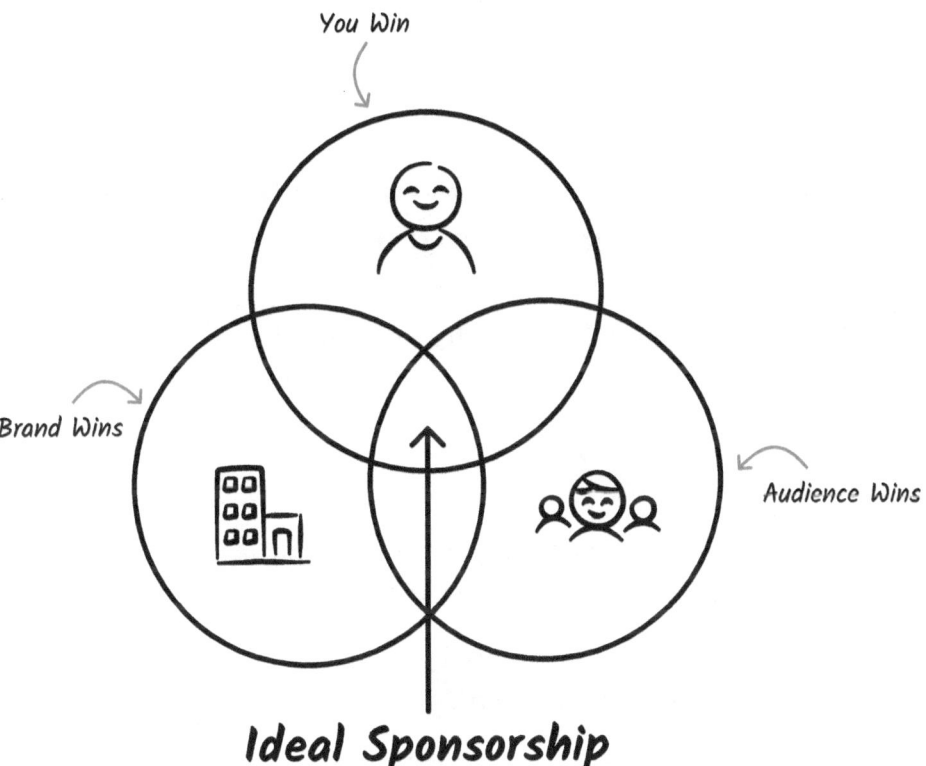

Maybe you're offering them a discount code. Maybe it's a seasonal promotion. Maybe you're exposing them to a product that will significantly improve their lives (survey data FTW!).

If it's clear from the beginning there's no "win" for your audience, you have to mandate that will be part of the deal (or walk away).

Brand offering a hybrid deal of $3K + a recurring 30% commission for anyone who signs up?

Tell them you'd like to *reduce your commission component* to 15% and offer a 15% discount to your audience.

Do you know how impressed the brand will be that you're so invested in ensuring this will succeed that you'll *accept less money?* Very.

Remember, every deal has to be Win-Win-Win.

Provide multiple packages instead of spitting back one number.

Brands often come inbound with a pre-defined Scope of Work (SOW) and Terms.

"How much for two posts, three months of paid usage rights, and three months of exclusivity?"

Most creators make the mistake of hitting reply to that email and spitting back one number like "$1,500."

Congrats, you've now encouraged the brand to compare you to every other partner they're vetting *exclusively on price.*

That your audience is super engaged, hangs on your every recommendation, and that your content quality crushes have become irrelevant.

The brand takes your rate, adds it to a giant spreadsheet containing all the creators they contacted, then picks the cheapest ones.

I want you to commit to something right here, right now.

Moving forward, whenever a brand asks how much you charge for a specific set of deliverables, *send them multiple packages instead.*

There are several important reasons to make this a cornerstone of your negotiation strategy.

Firstly, the brand might have found you on a social platform and assumed that was your primary presence. They might not even know you also have a newsletter with 5,000 of your most engaged audience members.

By presenting the brand with multiple packages outlining all the various ways you can amplify the campaign, you open the door to a deeper conversation.

Secondly, brands change their minds all the time. Even though they might say that this specific scope of work and terms are what they want, there could be flexibility.

Even though they asked for *two posts, three months of paid usage rights, and three months of exclusivity,* your Package 1 could propose a "stripped down" option such as *one post, no usage rights, and no exclusivity.*

Why can't you do this? (You can.)

Package 2 becomes *one post, one month of usage rights, and one month of exclusivity.*

Package 3 is now their original ask of *two posts, three months of paid usage rights, and three months of exclusivity.*

You should then add 1-3 more packages *above* that to stretch their imaginations!

These higher packages also serve as a price anchor, making Package 3 (their original SOW) feel like a good deal. Congratulations, you've just hacked the brand's brain.

One of the most challenging jobs a brand or agency has when planning a campaign is "Tetris-ing" all the partners' various rates to pull everything off within budget.

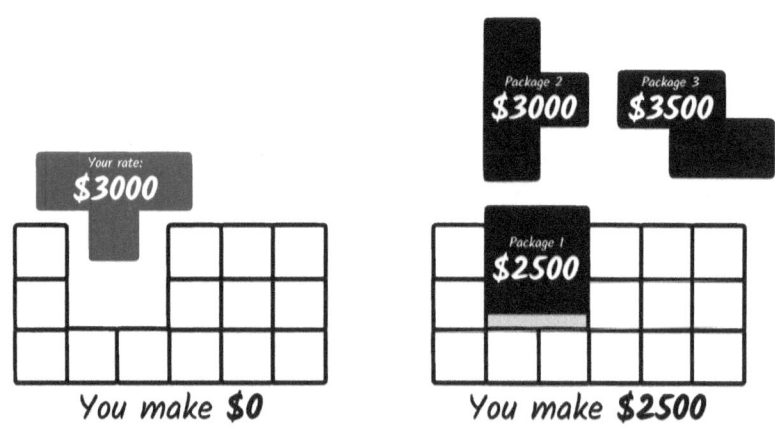

You make $0   You make $2500

Your goal should always be to ensure the brand has multiple ways to hire you if something happens, like a budget cut. Since you gave them flexibility, they'll still have the option to pick Package 1 or 2.

Now that your mind is racing over the power of packages, there's one structural mistake you must still avoid: making the only variance between each tier *quantity*.

Vary each package not by quantity but by the brand's objectives.

It's tempting to structure your packages in the following way:

Package 1:
- One post

Package 2:
- Two posts

Package 3:
- Three posts

To incentivize brands to select the top package, creators typically offer price concessions like a 10% discount.

To most brands, that's not very compelling.

Especially if you've never worked with a brand before, the likelihood of them hiring you for a long-term engagement with tons of deliverables is low.

Remember, they're accustomed to dealing with creators who aren't professional, lack timeliness, and are generally a pain in the butt.

So, naturally, they will be hesitant to commit to anything substantial until they have run one campaign with you.

However, you can take a different approach when designing your proposal that will help brands understand why hiring you for the most expensive package is in their best interest.

You must tie each package to the brand's goals.

Let's pretend you're on an initial discovery call with a prospective sponsor (or via email if you're petrified of calls).

You've done your research and asked them a bunch of questions to help you scope the partnership:
- What are your primary goals or success metrics for this collaboration? What would be a "win?"

- Tell me more about this product/service/launch! What do you find most exciting about it?
- Walk me through the competitive landscape. Do you feel you're the clear market leader, or are you fending off new entrants who are gaining ground?
- What are your primary sales channels? Online, retail, etc. Any supply chain issues?
- Have you ever worked with creators before? If so, what worked well? What didn't work so well? If you haven't worked with creators, why not? Do you have specific concerns or hesitations?
- [Insert any additional brand-, industry-, or niche-specific questions]

While all these insights will be helpful, learning the brand's objectives is the most important by far.

Very often, brands will tell you many different goals:

"*Awareness! More content! Sales!*"

Your *first job* is to educate them that accomplishing all those objectives with a single post or activation is unlikely.

Your *second job* then becomes outlining how each package in your proposal is tailored to their specific goals.

Here's the new way you're going to structure your packages:

What I Heard:
- *Goal 1: More eyeballs on our launch (Awareness)*
- *Goal 2: More Content (Repurposing)*
- *Goal 3: Sales (Conversions)*

Package 1
Achieves Goal 1

- 1 video
- Investment: $A

Package 2
Achieves Goal 1 and 2

- Includes everything in Package 1, PLUS:
- One podcast interview with a key brand representative
- Investment: $B

Package 3
Achieves Goal 1 and 2

- Includes everything in Package 2, PLUS:
- Five, thirty-second videos the brand can embed on its website or social media (organically)
- Investment: $C

Package 4
Achieves Goal 1 and 2

- Includes everything in Package 3, PLUS:
- Paid usage rights to use content from Package 3 in brand's advertising for 90 days
- Investment: $D

Package 5
Achieves Goal 1, 2, and 3

- Includes everything in Package 4, PLUS:
- 5 Dedicated newsletter blasts with an exclusive promo code
- Investment: $E

You'll likely notice that **the only way for the brand to accomplish all its objectives is to select the top package.**

Let's now address the elephant in the room:

What should the investment be for each package?

At this juncture, creators usually think the best thing to do is ask the brand, "What's your budget?"

They become frustrated when the brand is evasive or stonewalls and says...

> *"We don't have a budget."*

> *"Can you tell us your standard rates instead?"*

> *"We've never done this before, so can you tell us what's reasonable?"*

Putting aside whether the brand honestly doesn't know its budget (unlikely), there's a better question to ask that yields a far more helpful answer.

Ask for a budget *range* instead.

Don't ask brands for their budget; ask for a budget range.

At the end of your discovery call, if the brand somehow backs *you* into a corner and says, "So, how much do you typically charge for this kind of thing?" you must avoid coughing up a number you'll later cry/curse about in the shower.

Instead say,

"Thank you again for this call, as it's been super useful. I need time to think through everything, and then I'd love to get back to you with a custom proposal. Typically, I like to put together 3-4 packages to help you envision how we can bring this partnership to life. Do you have a sense of what I should set those 3-4 tiers at from a budget feasibility perspective?"

And then...*shut up.*

Don't say anything.

Lean into the silence.

I (as well as hundreds of my students) have used this exact method countless times, and one of two things will happen:

75% of the time the brand will tell you their budget range!

They'll say something like, "$1K, $2K, $3K" or, "$15K, $30K, $45K."

The brand feels more comfortable sharing because they now have wiggle room to modify the amount they'll ultimately pay you, if necessary.

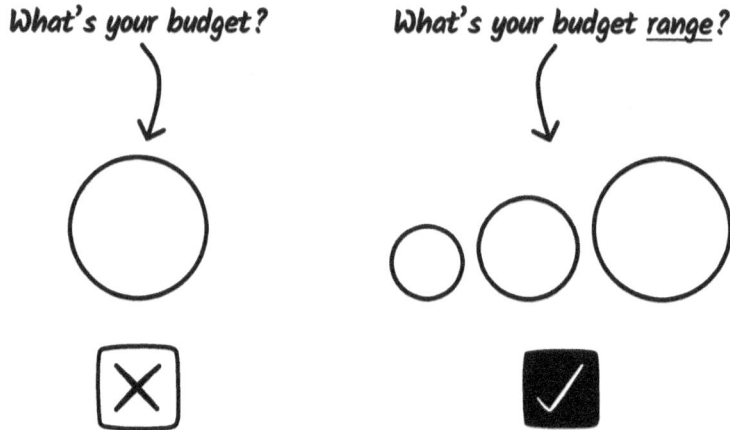

You'll also learn:
- Roughly where to set the minimum investment for Package 1
- Roughly where to set the investment for the top Package (it should be above the highest range they gave you!)
- How much time you should spend on the proposal (If I hear $10,000 vs. $100, I'm definitely putting in some extra hours)

But what about the 25% of the time when brands won't tell you their budget range?

My unscientific advice in these scenarios is to set the investment for Package 1 at your "Hell Yeah" number.

If the brand chooses Package 1, you should say, "Hell Yeah, let's do this!"

Not, "Aww bummer, I was hoping they'd pick Package 4. Now I have to do this."

The last thing you want is to start resenting the brand at the very outset of the collaboration.

"This is great, Justin, but I still don't know exactly how much to charge for the various things the brand asks for."

Ultimately, your price should factor in two main things: the brand's goals and the Scope of Work.

Calculate your price accounting for the brand's goals (A.R.C. framework) and the Scope of Work (D.U.E. Rule).

Let's pretend we're trying to price a single 90-second integration in a video post on a views-based platform.

The first thing you must do is calculate your Average Video Views (AVV).

To calculate your AVV, total the views for your last ten posts and divide by 10. If you have any significant outliers (e.g., a video with 150,000 views when your "typical" is 10,000), exclude that entirely from the calculation so you don't throw off the average.

The whole point of an average calculation is to reasonably anticipate how a *future* post would perform if the brand were to hire you.

For this example, let's say you calculate your AVV as 60,000.

Next we must assign a Cost-per-view, or CPV, relative to the Campaign Goal.

For benchmarking purposes, assume the following for views-based platforms:

Campaign Goal	Cost-per-view (CPV)
Awareness	~$0.10
Repurposing	~$0.065
Conversion	~$0.03

If the brand has indicated that the goal of this campaign is *Conversions,* the amount you would charge for *just the content creation* would be:

Content-only formula: AVV * CPV

Or 60,000 (AVV) * $0.03 (CPV) = $1,800.

> Note: *If the brand asks for a* **dedicated** *video (where the entire focus is on the brand), I recommend doubling the rate (total fee: $3,600).*

OK, back to the integrated example.

Now, let's imagine the brand's primary objective is *Awareness.* Instead of a $0.03 CPV, our formula becomes:

60,000 (AVV) * $0.10 (CPV) = $6,000.

That's more than 3x for an Awareness campaign vs. a Conversion campaign!

This is the primary reason you cannot price yourself in a vacuum using your audience size or reach, as the brand's objectives will massively affect the number you quote.

But wait, what if the brand wants exclusivity?

Exclusivity formula = Add an incremental 10% of the base investment for each 30 days.

If the brand asks for three months of exclusivity (from the integrated example), you would then charge:

($1,800 * 10%) * 3 months = $180 * 3 = $540

Total investment: $1,800 (content) + $540 (exclusivity) = $2,340

What if the brand only asks for usage rights to run advertising with your generated assets (but no exclusivity)?

You must first determine *where* they want to distribute it.

If the brand is asking you to send them the raw assets so they can upload them natively on their platforms (licensing), the formula becomes:

Licensing (On their platforms) = Add an incremental 15% of the base investment for every 30 days.

($1,800 * 15%) * 3 months = $270 * 3 = $810

Total investment: $1,800 (content) + $810 (licensing) = $2,610

If the brand also wants the ability to boost your native content (amplification), the formula becomes:

Amplification (On your platforms) = Add an incremental 25% of the base investment for each 30 days.

($1,800 * 25%) * 3 months = $450 * 3 = $1,350

Total investment: $1,800 (content) + $1,350 (licensing + amplification) = $3,150

What if they want the whole shebang? Exclusivity, licensing, and amplification rights for three months?

Add the Exclusivity and Paid Usage factors together (10% exclusivity + 25% paid usage = 35%).

($1,800 * 35%) * 3 months = $630 * 3 = $1,890

Total investment: $1,800 (content) + $1,890 (exclusivity + licensing + amplification) = $3,690

One very important "A-ha" I hope you have at this point is that, with many sponsorships, *the additional exclusivity and usage rights may exceed the investment for the content creation itself.*

In the example above, the additional rights are $1,890 while the content is $1,800.

If you feel uncomfortable employing this pricing strategy during an actual negotiation, rest assured that this structure is standard for most medium and large brands.

They're accustomed to paying a finite fee to a production company to generate creative assets they can use for much longer to run advertising campaigns.

Although I used a "video" for the sponsorship we calculated in the example above, similar formulas can be applied to every other content format.

Assume the following benchmarks for *impressions-based* platforms (social media, etc):

Campaign Goal	Cost-per-1,000 impressions (CPM)
Awareness	~$100
Repurposing	~$65
Conversion	~$30

Your Content-only formula then becomes: AI (Average Impressions) * CPM

E.g. (60,000 % 1,000) * $30 = $1,800

And assume the following benchmarks for *opens-based* platforms (newsletters, etc):

Campaign Goal	Cost-per-open (CPO)
Awareness	~$0.10
Repurposing	~$0.065
Conversion	~$0.03

Your Content-only formula then becomes: AO (Average Opens) * CPO

E.g. 60,000 * $0.03 = $1,800

As a reminder, I strongly recommend against granting perpetual usage rights unless you're paid a *lot* of money (at least 10x your typical investment) since the brand could theoretically exploit your name and likeness *forever*.

Note: *For event sponsorships (in-person or virtual), benchmarks vary wildly across industries, so your best bet is to refer to the previous section to ascertain the brand's feasible budget range.*

Pricing is an art and a science, so the formulas above should be treated as your baseline. If you calculate your numbers and they seem too low or too high, given the nature of your relationship with the sponsor or other deal dynamics, you should modify them until you're more comfortable.

However, many of my students have shared that sending uncomfortable numbers, *only for the brand to say, "YES!"* is what finally unlocked their negotiation fearlessness.

Note: *If you'd prefer to use my Sponsorship Pricing Calculator that incorporates these formulas, you can access it through my Brand Deal Wizard course: sponsormagnet.com/course*

Five scripts to help you counteroffer, double down, or walk away.

In an ideal world, the brand would trip over themselves to say "yes!" to the first number you throw out.

However, in almost all circumstances, they'll try to negotiate a lower amount.

Don't be insulted. This is just business, after all.

Instead, you can familiarize yourself with five common negotiation scenarios so you always know when to counteroffer, double down, or walk away.

Scenario #1: The brand won't budge on their rate

Solution: Communicate your strong "BATNA."

BATNA is a concept developed by Roger Fisher and William Ury of the Harvard Program on Negotiation. It means your "Best Alternative to a Negotiated Agreement."

It represents your best alternative option if the current negotiation fails.

When starting out and not making much money elsewhere, your BATNA is weak because you don't have other income streams to fall back on.

But you want to keep that private from the brand because it makes you seem desperate, with few options; so, of course, they'll lowball you.

However, building more diversified revenue streams empowers you to be more confident.

You know that if this deal doesn't work out it won't be the end of the world. And when brands sense that, it makes them want you more.

Here's a script for how to communicate that:

Hi [Name],

Thanks for sharing this context! We're motivated to find a way to make this work, but given our other commitments for this quarter, $X would be the required investment. Alternatively, if you'd be open to reducing the deliverables to 1 post and *confining the exclusivity term to 30 days, that would allow us to optimize our production calendar and make this work for $X-Y! Thoughts?*

Thanks,

[Your name]

One of the most uncomfortable things is calling a brand's bluff and saying,

"No. The investment is going to be $X. If you can't do $X, we can take a few things out of this and do it for $X-Y. Otherwise, best of luck with the campaign!"

How powerful would that feel?

Contrast that with decreasing your rate and the brand conceding nothing. Of course, you get the sponsorship (which is good), but now you have set a precedent in their minds that you will always come down on your rate and they have to give up nothing in return.

By the way, there is a deeper reason why we included the following sentence in the script:

"...that would allow us to optimize our production calendar and make this work for $X-Y!"

This is called "Labeling your Concessions." It was coined by Deepak Malhotra, another Harvard Negotiations professor.

Malhotra says giving a reason why you can concede on a particular deal point will help the other side understand why you're doing it.

In this case, now the brand understands that you take your schedule very seriously.

And, wow! If this creator has a production calendar, they must be legitimate.

There's no precedent now. If the brand returns to you in the future, they won't assume you'll lower your rate for no reason.

You were willing to do that in this particular situation for this specific reason.

But moving forward, you'll still have pricing power.

Scenario #2: The brand cares about things you don't

Solution: "Logroll" multiple issues

Logrolling, also coined by Malhotra, means you trade with the brand across multiple issues.

Almost without exception, the brand will care about very different things than you.

Here's how to do it:

Hi [Name],

Now that I understand how important it is to get multiple different cuts of the content so you can repurpose them across your various platforms, we should likely revisit the video length and the paid media licensing term.

[Insert explanation about why having shorter videos will be better to repurpose + longer paid rights will extend the lifespan of assets and increase ROI.] Thoughts?

Thanks,

[Your name]

If you plan to do a video in partnership with the brand, spending an extra thirty minutes making three to four extra cuts

(15-second vertical version, 30-second square version, etc.) would be trivial. But remember, the brand wants these.

On your side, the brand asked you to make the video at least 15 minutes long, which you know would tank its performance.

You can "logroll" these issues by saying,

> *"Knowing your priorities, it would be better to make the video closer to seven minutes. Not only will that improve the performance with my audience, but I can still make all the different cuts for you. We can extend the usage rights from three to 12 months to get more mileage out of the ad assets. The investment will be 2X, but this is a great solution to accomplish what you want."*

Scenario #3: The brand doesn't think you can deliver

Solution: Offer contingency contracts or guarantees

Instead of getting annoyed when brands are skeptical, put yourself in their shoes. Wouldn't you be cautious if you'd been burned in the past? In order to reassure them everything will go great, offer creative guarantees:

> *Hi [Name],*
>
> *Thanks for sharing your perspective here. I've got a few ideas that address these points, which will make this a win-win for both of us:*
>
> - *[insert responsiveness guarantee]*
> - *[insert flexibility guarantee]*
> - *[insert timeline guarantee]*

Let me know if you'd like me to send the different investment options to outline how we're both protected and ensure this partnership's success.

Thanks,

[Your name]

What's a responsiveness guarantee? Maybe the brand had a bad experience with a partner ghosting them or taking forever to get back to them. You say,

> *"I will commit to getting back to you within 48 hours, or if you have any revisions, I'll turn those around within 72 hours."*

What's a flexibility guarantee? Maybe the brand had a partner who threw an absolute stink when the brand asked them to make a few changes. You say,

> *"I will give you two rounds of revisions on my work, and if you need more we can build that into the investment options. I will commit to working together until you're thrilled with the outcome, no matter how many revisions it takes."*

What's a timeline guarantee? Does the brand need this partnership executed by a specific date, and they're not sure you can do it? Propose a bonus if you meet this expedited deadline. It doesn't even have to be a bonus! You can say,

> *"X will be the investment if I hit this deadline, and if I don't, you can pay me X-Y."*

In your head, you know you're going to hit that deadline no matter what, but the brand suddenly feels like it can justify paying you more money.

By the way, this stuff is *not* theoretical!

Here's a screenshot from an actual deal my wife and I did:

9.	FEE	Base Rate: $14,500 USD
		Bonus: $3,265 USD
		"Bonus" will be paid upon the condition that all Works and Social Post Assets are completed and delivered to no later than the Works and Social Post Assets are not delivered by only the "Base Rate" will be paid to Collaborator.
		Total Rate (if Bonus is included): $18,125 USD

Scenario #4: The brand says they don't have the budget

Solution: "Stretch" the sponsorship

Remember the creator who turned a $5,000 sponsorship offer into $60,000 at the beginning of this chapter?

Here's how to phrase it:

Hi [Name],

Thanks for letting me know about your budget constraints. Would it help if we stretched the partnership over 2-3 months with the ability to pay in monthly installments? I'm confident this collaboration will be a big success so I'm motivated to find ways to make it happen.

Thoughts?

Thanks,

[Your name]

Scenario #5: The brand asks to add something small

Solution: Do it for free!

You don't need to charge the brand extra every single time they come back to you with a small request. In fact, it reinforces their opinion of you when you don't.

> *Hi [Name],*
>
> *Thanks for letting me know that the brand hoped I could create a post in my private community announcing our partnership. My primary motivation is to establish a great (and long!) relationship with you and your agency, so I'd be happy to do that at no additional cost.*
>
> *Looking forward to the next steps!*
>
> *Thanks,*
>
> *[Your name]*

Doing something like this accomplishes a few things at once.

First, it makes you seem like a nice person and someone they'll want to work with again.

Second, it will psychologically make your contact want to reciprocate.

Maybe they'll go to bat for you internally and try to get you a higher rate than they may have budgeted. Or go to bat for you on a future deal.

I hope it's clear by now that all these things are in service of forging healthy, long-term relationships with brands so that any time an opportunity slides across their desk where you'd even *remotely* be a good fit, they'll instantly think of you.

At the same time, you must develop the fortitude to walk away from specific sponsorships.

Maybe the brand is offering low compensation. Maybe they're being rude or challenging during the negotiation. Maybe you have a feeling in your stomach that your audience will revolt if you take the deal.

You can't ignore your gut on these things. Better to walk away from a short-term payday than destroy your long-term credibility.

Ten scripts to handle the "free stuff" conundrum.

There's a time and place for doing small things for free (e.g., at the tail end of a negotiation).

However, many brands will explicitly state they only offer gifted products or free access in exchange for promotion.

Now, I know a free six-pack of sparkling strawberry seltzer sounds awesome, but last I checked, landlords and banks don't accept delicious drinks as payment (if you know one that does, hit me up).

It's also a big mistake to say, "I'm only focusing on paid sponsorships right now," then slam the door in their face. You must recognize that outreach as an early signal of interest.

Your task now becomes educating the brand on why compensating you makes good business sense.

Let's talk through 10 different scenarios and how to respond with confidence.

Scenario #1: The brand offers free products or services but doesn't require you to post

Solution: Propose a specific Statement of Work (SOW)

Hi [Name],

The product looks really cool and I appreciate that offer!

I know you mentioned I'm not required to post about it but I would love to create the following:

- *One 90-second video integration*
- *One social media post (30-second cut-down of video)*
- *Grant you ad rights to all assets for three months*

Would you be interested in that? Let me know if you can pull from a different budget for a collaboration like this.

Thanks!

[Your name]

125

What do I mean by "pull from a different budget"?

Brands typically allocate different "buckets" of money to different marketing strategies.

The strategy you've found yourself caught in is the "earned media" bucket.

Earned media is where the brand takes a "spray and pray" approach. It contacts hundreds of people to see who will talk about its products for free.

And they're going to do that all day long. You can't get mad! That's just the way it is and will always be.

But your goal is to get them to remove you from the "earned media" bucket and put you in the "paid media" bucket.

Let me ask you a question.

If a brand runs social media ads, do you think these platforms let them do that for free?

No, they don't. Brands have to pay for that privilege.

The faster you can convince the brand to shift its mindset about what you're bringing to the table (e.g., content production *and* an organic distribution channel), the easier it will be to convince them to compensate you.

Scenario #2: The brand's Public Relations (PR) team or agency offers a shipment of free stuff in exchange for promotion

Solution: Find out if their team is responsible for paid media

Hi [Name],

This looks amazing, and my audience would love this!

Out of curiosity, is your team also handling paid media for this campaign?

If you expedite the package to me, I can quickly create a compelling 15-second video highlighting this initiative that the brand can use to extend the reach and visibility.

Let me know if that's of interest and I can send over the investment.

Thanks!

[Your name]

Focusing on the quick turnaround is imperative because most brand campaigns have a short flight (duration), such as 30 or 60 days.

That's why your reply must emphasize that your specialty is speed. The brand doesn't have time to spend three weeks negotiating with you and another four weeks waiting for content delivery. By that time, the campaign will likely be over.

Scenario #3: The brand invites you to join their affiliate program

Solution: Make them question their current strategy

Hi [Name],

Thanks for sending that info on your affiliate program!

Out of curiosity, how do you currently source social media content?

Also, do your affiliates grant you rights to use their content for ads?

I specialize in collaborations with a flat investment, so let me know if you'd like to discuss how I can help you get a better ROI from your influencer strategy.

Thanks!

[Your name]

This will be music to a brand's ears because they're all concerned with getting a return on their investment.

Most creators shy away from this topic because they aren't confident they can earn a return for the brand.

But remember, ROI is not always about how many sales you generate.

The brand might think, *"Actually, we're not getting usage rights from our affiliates for the content they're creating. That's a great idea. Let's talk to this person about how they do it and whether the cost would make sense."*

Scenario #4: The brand offers you a gift card as payment

Solution: Accept it to test the product but clarify that promotion requires compensation

Hi [Name],

Thanks so much for the offer!

If you'd like to send a gift card first, that will allow me time to test out your product and confirm it will be an excellent fit for my audience (I'm sure it will)!

Then, if you'd like me to do a comprehensive promotion, we can discuss the investment.

What do you think?

[Your name]

Rather than being insulted by a brand's gift card offer, you can flip this around in your mind and get excited! Brands love working with authentic fans and *don't* love working with people who view collaborations as one-and-done transactions.

Accepting the gift while clearly stating there are no promotion "strings" attached could lead to a compensated partnership later on.

Scenario #5: The brand says gifted first, then paid if post performs well

Solution: Explain that one post isn't enough to determine success

Hi [Name],

I appreciate you sharing this! In my experience, it takes several posts to measure the success of a partnership.

For example, repeatedly illustrating to my audience that I'm continuing to love and use a product builds credibility and increases purchase intent.

Also, if we partnered through June for monthly posts, we could meet periodically and analyze the results from each post and, if needed, change our approach.

I'm sure you've found that the same long-term outlook is required to see success when running ads on social media.

Can I send over a few investment options for what a collaboration like this could look like?

[Your name]

The key here is drawing the analogy once again to social media ads that virtually every brand is running.

Predicting what will do well when they run ads is often challenging.

For example, when I ran my agency, a giant phone carrier hired us to execute a campaign with several social media influencers. As part of the deal, they asked us to create a bunch of cut-downs of the content they could repurpose as ads.

Most videos were super polished and professional, while others looked like they were filmed on a potato.

I was sure the glossy ads would perform the best, but what do you think happened?

The low-quality selfie video ads crushed everything else by a considerable margin.

Your goal in this scenario is to help the brand understand that multiple posts are often needed to assess a partnership's success accurately.

Scenario #6: The brand says the product is expensive so that should be "enough" compensation

Solution: Make them drool over your audience and have FOMO (Fear of Missing Out)

Hi [Name],

I understand where you're coming from.

This collaboration will perform well because my audience regularly messages me when they've purchased [similar products or products at a comparable price point] that I've shared.

Check out the attached screenshots for a few examples. I've also attached my demographics and additional psychographic research I've conducted so you can see how my audience aligns with the types of consumers you're trying to reach.

With this in mind, what budget can you allocate to our partnership?

Thanks!

[Your name]

If you're not collecting screenshots when your audience tells you they've purchased something you recommended, start *now*.

Remember, brands don't want to work with you because you're terrific. That might be *part* of the reason, but it's mainly because they want to access your audience, which is filled with potential future customers of their brand.

So, you need to agitate that FOMO and (tactfully) say,

"I know your product's expensive, but you've got to pay the toll if you want to talk to my audience. By the way, here are some screenshots and data to back up that it'll be worth it."

Scenario #7: The brand asks to repost your content

Solution: Share your excitement and ask reasonable questions

Hi [Name],

It's great to connect, and I'm honored you liked my post. [insert sentence reemphasizing why you love their brand/ product so much]

I'm absolutely interested in granting your brand the right to repurpose my content!

Can you share a few details, such as:

- *How long will the usage term be?*
- *Are you looking to repost it organically on your social handles or website?*
- *Are you also looking to secure paid media rights?*

I'd also be open to granting boosting/allow-listing rights if it interests you.

Let me know what budget range you've set aside for this, and we can discuss next steps.

Thanks!

[Your name]

99% of the time, you'll never see any real growth or traction from getting "exposure" on a brand's platforms.

Instead, treat this scenario as a clear signal the brand sees value in your work and quickly pivot to a more comprehensive partnership proposal.

Scenario #8: The brand reposts your content without asking you and does/doesn't credit you

Solution: Let them know that is something they have to compensate you for

Hi [Name],

I'm so glad you enjoyed my video about [your brand/product/ service] so much that you reposted it!

Repurposing my content requires an investment, so can you let me know what budget you've set aside to secure those rights?

I also have a few collaboration ideas featuring [your brand/ product/service] I'd love to share!

Are you free on Thursday at 1 pm to chat?

Thanks!

[Your name]

Brands will likely get a big lump in their throats over this bit: "What budget have you set aside for this..." because they're going to think, "Yikes. We didn't think we needed to secure the rights to repurpose this."

Way better to engage with and compensate you than risk legal action or public blowback.

Scenario #9: The brand says they've never worked with partners before

Solution: Flex your expertise and offer to help them with higher-level strategy

Hi [Name],

Thanks for connecting with me about this opportunity!

It's super smart of you to consider adding influencer market- ing to your advertising strategy.

I've worked with many brands and companies in a similar [category/industry/niche], so I have a lot of experience with best practices and mistakes you should avoid.

I can help you promote your [brand/product/service] and be an ongoing resource as you build your partnership program.

Are you free on Wednesday at 10 am to hop on a call?

Thanks,

[Your name]

I can guarantee that no one else will offer to help the brand think through its high-level strategy in this way.

It communicates that you're invested in the outcome of their advertising efforts and reduces the brand's anxiety about paying you a lot of money.

Scenario #10: The brand says other people did it for free, so why not you?

Solution: Differentiate yourself by explaining your approach

Hi [Name],

It's awesome to hear that others have been willing to do it for free. However, my approach to collaboration is quite a bit different.

Working with key partners like [your brand] is a core priority for my business, and as such I maintain a high level of service.

For example:

- *< 48 hours response time on all email communications*
- *Concepts provided in advance of production for [your brand's] feedback*
- *< 72 hours turnaround time on all revisions, if necessary*

- *Ample flexibility when any issues arise regarding timeline or other partnership logistics*
- *Every concept and strategy is explicitly customized to achieve [your brand's] objectives*
- *We can meet monthly or quarterly to assess the status/ performance of the partnership and make course corrections as necessary*

Let me know if you're free on Tuesday at 10 am to chat through ways we could optimize your influencer marketing strategy.

Thanks!

[Your name]

It doesn't feel great when brands try to gaslight you. I get it.

But, rather than getting defensive, assuming the brand doesn't know any better is more productive.

For example, what if the brand had already contacted ten other people who all gladly accepted the free products without any pushback?

Until I've successfully snuck this book onto the required reading list for every brand's corporate training program, you might be the very first person who offers to educate them on why compensating partners is a wise move.

Maintain objectivity by using the R.E.L.A.Y. negotiation framework.

We've now established that when a brand decides to run a marketing campaign, they have a particular marketing objective in mind.

They put together a plan outlining the internal and external partners they need because they can't do it alone.

They dream of finding someone like you and saying, "We'd like to pass the baton to you."

Searching for partners sucks. Help them end their search with you!

You're both on the same team. You're not fighting each other. This is not a battle.

You're running the same race. They want to hand it off to you so you can take it to the finish line.

And guess what?

They're going to pay you money for this! In fact, they'll pay you lots of money if you can make their lives easier.

Brands want to relax. They don't want to be stressed about whether they'll achieve their marketing objectives.

So if you can tell them, "I got this, don't worry. You don't need to micromanage me because I'm a professional. I got it from here..."

...They'll fall head over heels for you.

But if you're ever feeling stuck, here's the R.E.L.A.Y. negotiation framework you can use at any point in your negotiations to figure out what to do or say next.

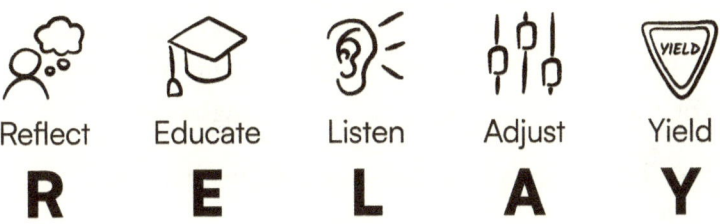

Reflect	Educate	Listen	Adjust	Yield
R	**E**	**L**	**A**	**Y**

Reflect

First, when the brand or agency says something you don't understand or didn't expect, **Reflect** on why you think they're asking for this.

They may be asking for more deliverables than you expected or for you to say things in your work that you think are weird. Think about why that might be.

"Ahh, of course, because brands take abject pleasure in trying to stress me out!"

Let's be real - it's almost certainly *not* that.

Educate

Next, **Educate** the brand and explain your position with confidence.

Don't simply concede and say, *"OK, I'll do whatever it takes to make it work."*

No. If the brand says you need to add four different calls to action, you explain to them how that will substantially affect the performance of your work (and here's what we should do instead).

Listen

Next, **Listen.** After you educate the brand on your position, they'll either say, "OK, we trust you, we can make that work..." or, "No. You must do it our way, or it'll be the highway."

You must be objective and open-minded, not emotional and entitled.

Remember, what separates professionals who get hired repeatedly for projects from amateurs who only ever get one-off sponsorships is understanding that this is a *business transaction*.

You must have empathy for your *partner* throughout this *partnership*.

Adjust

Then, you have to **Adjust.** You must decide whether you're going to:

A. Modify your position based on these new conditions or explanations from the brand or

B. Stand your ground

This will be context-specific based on your current rapport with the brand or agency, whether this is the first sponsorship you've done with them, and so many other factors.

Yield

Finally, and this might surprise you; you're going to **Yield.**

That's right. You're *not* going to take every single last dollar off the table.

Because what happens in that scenario? Even though the deal gets done, the brand or the agency has a sour taste in their mouths.

And now you must execute this partnership together where they're already on the defensive.

However, if you pull up slightly before the final agreement and concede something minor, they'll think, "Wow! That was awesome of them to do that!" They'll feel the deal was fair and be more willing to work with you through any issues that arise during the execution phase.

And you're going to vastly increase the chances of getting repeat business.

R.E.L.A.Y. Negotiation Framework
- **Reflect** – why are they saying this?
- **Educate** – explain your position with confidence
- **Listen** – be objective and open-minded
- **Adjust** – modify your position based on new conditions
- **Yield** – "Pull up" before final agreement

One of the critical mindset shifts in negotiations is that you will make a different amount of money on every single deal.

Like the stock market, having a well-diversified portfolio means some dividends will be more lucrative than others.

It's the same with sponsorships. You can't get hung up on insignificant details in every negotiation so don't waste your time arguing over pennies if the brand's offer is fair. Just accept it and move on to the next one.

Again, like a stock portfolio, what matters is not the individual deals per se; it's about how much money you're bringing in consistently.

Of course, my goal is to help you make a lot more money on each sponsorship, but it's essential to have the broader perspective that, in two years, you won't remember whether a company paid you 10% less or 20% more than you usually get. You'll remember how much you made the entire year.

So, don't get fixated on trivial things that can cause your relationship with the brand or the agency to deteriorate.

Avoid "Resulting" when a negotiation fails.

One of the most lucrative sponsorships that April and I ever landed was with a pharmaceutical brand for $50,000.

We forged the deal via the brand's advertising agency and developed a great relationship with them throughout the partnership. So, when that agency returned to us six months later with a new opportunity for a different pharmaceutical brand, we ensured that our proposal included options around $50,000.

Unfortunately, the agency informed us that this campaign's maximum budget was $7,000, so we politely declined.

It'd be easy to kick ourselves for overbidding so drastically, but given the Statement of Work and previous price precedent, *it was the right decision* to anchor our packages around $50,000.

Annie Duke, former professional poker player and author of *Thinking in Bets*, defines this tendency to evaluate the quality of our decisions based on the outcomes as "Resulting."

It's common to have a great outcome and laud yourself for making a great decision. However, how much of it was good luck or good timing?

Similarly, bad outcomes don't necessarily stem from bad decision-making.

To be clear, walking away from $7,000 sucked, but we didn't lose sleep over it since it was the right call (and we maintained our future pricing power).

Duke also posits that life is much more like poker than chess.

In chess, all information is accessible (you know the positions of your opponent's pieces at all times) and there's very little luck involved (other than your opponent's errors).

However, in poker you're dealing with incomplete information (your opponents' cards) and quite a bit of luck (the cards still in the dealer's deck).

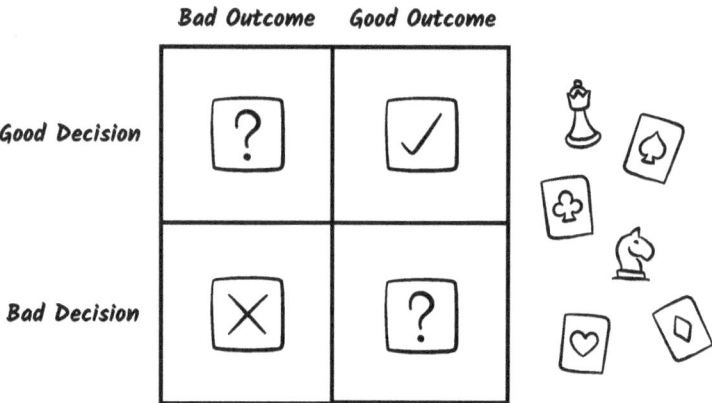

When a sponsorship negotiation fails, remember that a brand rarely turns over their poker hand and tells you why they're passing.

While you should still be introspective and analyze how you can improve on the next negotiation, don't abandon a good strategy if you conclude your approach was sound.

Estimate the "Expected Value" of your sponsorships to forecast revenue more accurately.

It's human nature to be bummed when a deal doesn't work out, but it especially sucks if you were counting on that money to pay essential bills.

This is why it's critical to start calculating the *Expected Value* of all your potential sponsorships to have a more accurate revenue figure.

For example, let's say you're negotiating three separate deals and quoted each brand the following:

- Deal X: $1,000
- Deal Y: $3,000
- Deal Z: $5,000

You can assign the following probabilities that each deal will close based on the context and dynamics of each negotiation.

- Deal X: 90%
- Deal Y: 40%
- Deal Z: 15%

Instead of subconsciously banking on $9,000 worth of sponsorships, we can calculate the *Expected Value* of these three opportunities:

- Deal X: 90% * $1,000 = $900
- Deal Y: 40% * $3,000 = $1,200
- Deal Z: 15% * $5,000 = $750

Total Expected Value (Deal X + Deal Y + Deal Z) = $2,850

This figure is a much more accurate estimation of the revenue you can expect from these three negotiations.

We need to do a more complex example because, remember, you're no longer spitting back one number when a brand asks how much you charge. You're sending packages!

Imagine this scenario where you send three brands three packages each and assign a different probability to *each package:*

Deal 1:

- Package A: $1,000 (80%)
- Package B: $2,000 (15%)
- Package C: $3,000 (5%)

Deal 2:

- Package A: $3,000 (5%)
- Package B: $5,000 (90%)
- Package C: $7,000 (5%)

Deal 3:

- Package A: $10,000 (50%)
- Package B: $20,000 (25%)
- Package C: $30,000 (25%)

The Total Expected Value becomes:

	Deal 1	Deal 2	Deal 3
	Package A: $1,000 (80%) Package B: $2,000 (15%) Package C: $3,000 (5%)	Package A: $3,000 (5%) Package B: $5,000 (90%) Package C: $7,000 (5%)	Package A: $10,000 (50%) Package B: $20,000 (25%) Package C: $30,000 (25%)
Expected Value of each deal	$1,000 * 80% + $2,000 * 15% + $3,000 * 5% = $800 + $300 + $150 = $1,250	$3,000 * 5% + $5,000 * 90% + $7,000 * 5% = $150 + $4,500 + $350 = $5,000	$10,000 * 50% + $20,000 * 25% + $30,000 * 25% = $5,000 + $5,000 + $7,500 = $17,500

Total Expected Value **$23,750**

Awesome, right?

Of course, you may win or lose all three negotiations, too!

However, reframing your expectations and understanding the power of probability will give you more clarity and objectivity when growing your sponsorship business.

Speaking of clarity and objectivity, it's time to move on to Step 3 (Contract) to discuss how to protect yourself after successfully negotiating a sponsorship.

Bonus:

Claim the free bonuses from this chapter
at ***sponsormagnet.com/negotiate***

- 5 scripts to help you counteroffer, double down, or walk away
- 10 scripts to handle the "free stuff" conundrum
- Campaign Goals Cheat Sheet (A.R.C. framework)

PLEASE READ BEFORE PROCEEDING:

If you've already gotten value from this book, would you mind taking 60 seconds to write a quick review?

I have this ridiculous goal to get Sponsor Magnet into the hands of 100,000 creators and there's no way I'll be able to do it without your help.

Plus, I'll give you a high-five the next time I see you in person.

Deal?

Simply visit sponsormagnet.com/review

Thank you!

Justin

STEP 3

Contract

Note: I'm not a lawyer and what I'm about to tell you shouldn't be construed as legal advice. You should always consult a lawyer before entering into an agreement.

In 2012, a fashion marketplace approached April with an incredible opportunity to be one of their first ambassadors.

In exchange for encouraging her YouTube viewers to sign up, the company promised April an ongoing 25% revenue share for all purchases from referred users.

The company seemed legitimate, with news articles from prominent outlets detailing the millions of dollars of venture capital they had raised.

April and I talked it over and decided to go for it.

When we asked the company if they could send a contract, they said, "A contract is going to slow everything down; we don't need to worry about that."

We felt uneasy, but since we were still inexperienced in negotiating, we thought that was normal. Plus, we feared that if we pushed back the brand might change its mind and not want to collaborate anymore!

So we didn't bring up the contract again (oops).

Another thing: when we asked the company if they had a dashboard we could log into once the partnership launched that would reflect our performance, they said, "We don't have one yet because this program is so new."

Again, we didn't push it (double oops).

At this point, you're probably thinking the deal went off without a hitch and there were no unforeseen consequences whatsoever. Thanks for always being so positive, dear reader!

April proceeded to film a dedicated YouTube video promoting the marketplace and, within the first few days, the company told us she drove *thousands of new sign-ups*. Not just that; her viewers started messaging her, sharing everything they had purchased from the site.

April was ecstatic! We started fantasizing about how much commission she might generate. Plus, since it was an ongoing deal, we wondered, "What might this generate *every month?!*"

After a few weeks, we emailed the company and asked if they could send us a report with projected commissions.

No response.

Followed up a week later.

No response.

We started to freak out a little bit.

I found the phone number of one of the founders from our initial conversation and decided to call him.

When the founder picked up the phone, he seemed dodgy. I asked him about the commission report, and he said he didn't handle those details. Then he gave me the email address of someone else at the company.

I gave him the benefit of the doubt and emailed the new contact.

Nothing.

Followed up.

Crickets.

By now, several months had passed and we were pretty upset. I called the founder repeatedly, and it went straight to voicemail every time.

This was such a weird experience because I consider myself an extremely honest person (I'm an Eagle Scout, after all). So it was inconceivable to me that someone wouldn't honor their end of a deal, even if there were no contracts to back it up.

Then, one morning, a news article popped into my inbox: the company behind the fashion marketplace just declared bankruptcy.

My heart sank.

As I read further, everything started clicking into place.

The "amazing brand ambassador opportunity" was likely a desperate attempt to save the company from bankruptcy.

We lost a lot from that terrible experience, but more importantly, we *gained* a lot of knowledge about what we'd do differently moving forward.

I wish I could say we never made any more contract mistakes after that, but...we did.

It took a solid five more years and 100+ deals to figure out how to finally protect ourselves.

And now it's time to pass those learnings on to you.

Common mistakes and pitfalls with contracts.

- Using an email thread or DM as "proof" of the collaboration
- Not understanding the terms you're agreeing to and signing the contract anyway
- Getting into legal trouble if you breach the contract

One of the most intimidating parts of doing sponsorships can be receiving a complicated contract from a brand.

The language might be confusing, the document super long, and perhaps the brand is pressuring you to sign it on a quick timeline.

The following internal monologue is what usually happens for most people:

"I need to find a lawyer."

"I don't know any lawyers."

"Aren't lawyers expensive?"

"Meh, it's probably fine. I'll just sign it."

I get it.

Hiring a lawyer might eat all your profit, especially if the sponsorship isn't for much money.

Sure, everything might go fine. It probably will go fine the first few times.

But doing sponsorships without contracts is like petting a koala. It's harmless until you get your face mauled.

An even more intimidating situation is when a brand asks *you* to send them a contract.

Especially when a brand is newer to doing sponsorships, they may look to you for guidance on memorializing the partnership.

My sincere advice is that one of the best investments you can make in yourself and your business is to hire a lawyer to create a boilerplate contract template for you.

The bulk of the contract will contain all the language that protects you (and will never change). The only page you touch for each deal is the Statement of Work at the end.

You'll simply fill out the SOW with all the deal points you agreed to on the phone with the brand or via email.

> *"But Justin, again, this deal isn't large enough to justify hiring a lawyer."*

Imagine you wanted to start any other business. How about an ice cream shop?

There are lots of costs you would need to expend before you could sell a single ice cream cone.

Rent, labor, insurance, appliances, ingredients, and much more.

What are *your* costs as a creator, influencer, or entrepreneur?

I'd venture they're considerably less than a brick and mortar store.

Maybe a computer, software, cameras, Internet? Therapy for that one time someone left a comment on your video saying you have no talent and should just give up? (Looking at you, @TrollKing8935147)

If you want sponsorships to grow into a lucrative, recurring revenue stream, hiring a lawyer to create a boilerplate contract template is a good investment.

Before we get into how to familiarize ourselves with various contract terms, I must warn you of one colossal mistake: **When you receive a contract, if you notice a clause where the brand is asking for something you suddenly feel should cost more money, *do not try to return to the negotiating table.***

This is a terrible idea for many reasons.

First, it makes you look bad because it seems like you don't know what you're doing.

Second, and more importantly, it makes your brand or agency contact look bad.

Before sending you the contract, they went to their boss or client and said, "Great news, Justin is locked in at $XYZ!" The boss then said, "Awesome, ask the legal team to create a contract."

When you ask for more money, your contact has to go back and say, "I know I told you Justin was locked in, but now he's demanding more money."

You look greedy. Your contact looks like an idiot. Their boss now thinks they're sloppy. To top it all off, the legal team is now mad that they must do extra work.

Not a great start to the partnership.

Instead, from this point forward, you must ask every detail you can think of about the deal structure, deliverables, and terms *in advance* so there are never any "gotchas" when the contract arrives.

While I strongly suggest you always seek legal advice before signing any contract, I also understand that you're probably going to ignore me at times.

So, at the very least, let's familiarize you with the most important clauses and language you need to know to protect yourself.

Execute the agreement using the correct "party," so there's a distinction between you and your business.

You'll be referenced in a sponsorship contract in two main places.

The first will usually be in the opening paragraph where it says something like, "This contract is entered into by and between the Agency on behalf of its client, the Brand, and [Your name]."

If you have a legal structure for your business (e.g., LLC or S Corporation in the U.S.), then *that* needs to be listed under "[Your name]."

Instead of signing the contract as Justin Moore, you'll use your business entity for the services of (f/s/o) Justin Moore.

| Justin Moore | ACME INC. F/S/O Justin Moore |

Note: *if you haven't formalized your business legally yet or are wondering whether you need one, contact a local lawyer and/or tax advisor.*

The second place you'll be referenced in a sponsorship contract is where you sign your name at the very end.

You must ensure that the "party" or "entity" they're referencing in this signatory area matches the opening paragraph.

While this might seem unnecessary or overly formal, there are two reasons you should care.

1. When the brand or agency is ready to write a check to you for the sponsorship, their finance team will usually ask for your tax form. All your paperwork must match for them to issue the payment.

2. In the unlikely event you ever get sued by someone in your audience who used the shampoo you recommended and their hair fell out, they can't come after your personal assets.

Clarify the duration of the agreement so everyone is on the same page.

Sometimes, brands or agencies will add to the contract that the Term/duration of the sponsorship will be much longer than you expected.

Even worse, the Term might be open-ended.

It might say, "This agreement will persist until canceled by both parties upon 30 days' written notice."

Not OK.

Every sponsorship you do should have a defined length.

If there's no clause spelling that out, ask the brand or agency to add one.

Verify the deliverables, usage rights, and exclusivity terms match what was agreed so you don't accidentally commit to a very different deal.

If you've ever been in a negotiation that has gone back and forth many times, you know that brands or agencies often make mistakes when listing the deliverables in the contract.

But it's *your job* to double-check everything so you don't accidentally agree to twice as much work.

While it doesn't happen often, I've heard of situations where people signed contracts not realizing they misunderstood how much the brand wanted them to do. Once they realized this, they asked the brand, who said, "Sorry, you already signed it."

Do yourself a favor, take two minutes and verify that the contract clearly states what you will deliver.

Another section to verify is the ownership and usage rights.

Do you own the content, or does the brand? Typically, you should always own the content and provide a non-exclusive license to the brand for a particular duration.

If the brand wants to outright "own" your content (sometimes called "Work for Hire"), that should cost more (~3-10x).

Speaking of things that should cost more, always verify the usage rights are correctly articulated.

Here's an actual excerpt from one of our past contracts with a brand:

> "*[You] hereby grant to Client, and to Client's senior executives, the right to use, share, and promote Sponsored Posts, including, without limitation, via social media platforms (whether owned and/or operated by Client and/or a third party) without the need to remove such Sponsored Posts after the Term. Additionally, from on or about the first post published by [You] through [Date], Client is granted permission to 'allowlist' the Sponsored Posts, meaning when [You] post about the campaign, Client can apply paid support against your Sponsored Post to reach a broader audience. [You] agree to provide all required documents and permissions necessary for Client to allowlist, including, but not limited to, making Client an ad manager on the social account.*"

I know, not exactly a page-turner. When reviewing language like this, ask yourself, "Did I grant the brand paid media rights during the negotiation?"

If you did...

- Was it licensing (on the brand's platforms) or amplification (on your platforms)?

- What Term/duration did you agree to?
- Is that Term/duration accurately expressed in the contract?

If you didn't...

- How can the brand modify the contract to reflect the proper usage rights?

And remember, I strongly recommend against granting the brand usage rights to your work *in perpetuity*. That would enable them to exploit it in paid advertising...forever. The only time when it's acceptable to have the word "perpetual" in your contract is when you're allowing the brand to showcase your work for internal purposes:

> *"[You] grant Company and Client a perpetual, nonexclusive, irrevocable, worldwide, royalty-free, fully paid-up, transferrable license, with the unlimited right to grant sublicenses, to use the Content for non-commercial corporate, internal, and archival purposes; client presentations; award submissions; and case studies."*

Exclusivity is also critical to verify.

Here's another excerpt from the same contract I mentioned above:

> *"[You] agree that you will not, at any time during the Term and for six (6) months thereafter, render, participate, or perform any services of any kind directly or indirectly for any other company, group, organization, or product related to [Client's product category], including but not limited to [list of Client's competitors]."*

When reviewing language like this, ask yourself, "Did I discuss with the brand that I wouldn't work with their competitors?"

If you did...
- What Term/duration did you agree to?
- Is that Term/duration accurately expressed in the contract?
- What product category did you agree to?

If you didn't...
- How can you ask the brand to modify the contract to reflect that there's no exclusivity?

I once spoke with a creator on the verge of tears who didn't realize they had agreed to long and confining exclusivity with a huge brand.

They then forged a deal with a direct competitor, produced the content, and published it.

The original brand saw this, freaked out, and threatened legal action.

The creator had to remove the new post quickly and had no choice but to terminate the deal with the competitor.

You must avoid reputational damage like that at all costs.

Articulate what qualifies as a revision so you don't do extra work.

When you work with brands on sponsored projects, a large percentage of the time they will want to see drafts of your work before you publish or activate.

This is so they can provide feedback and request revisions if your discussion or depiction of the brand or its products was inaccurate.

Revisions are reasonable for brands to ask for (we'll discuss how to handle feedback gracefully in Chapter 6).

However, what's not reasonable is a brand claiming they're entitled to *unlimited* revisions.

This is why you must distinguish between *re-edits* and *re-shoots*. If you create video content, re-edits are simple revisions to a video or easy updates to a social media caption.

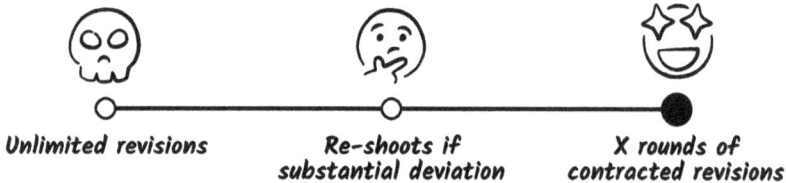

Unlimited revisions   Re-shoots if substantial deviation   X rounds of contracted revisions

The brand is not justified in saying, "We didn't like that plant in your background, so you need to reshoot the whole video."

Instead, request that the brand modifies the revision language as follows:

> "[You] agree to up to two rounds of re-edits. However, re-shoots are only permitted if [You] substantially deviate from the Approved Creative Brief and Approved Concept. Incremental compensation will be mutually negotiated if additional re-edits or re-shoots are required."

Ask for mutual indemnification and limitation of liability so you're protected, not just the brand.

Many sponsorship contracts have language such as:

> *"[You] will indemnify and hold harmless [Client] against all liability to third parties arising from or in connection with [Your] material uncured breach of this agreement."*

Why is the brand the only one who gets to be protected?

It's perfectly reasonable to request this to read instead,

> ***"Each Party** will indemnify and hold harmless the **Other Party** against all liability to third parties..."*

Similarly, having language limiting your liability is paramount in the event of legal action:

"The combined, aggregate liability hereunder shall not exceed the compensation payable to [You] under this Agreement."

Add language that governs termination, venue, and morality so you're still compensated if something goes wrong.

Sometimes, issues arise during a sponsorship that are not your fault and force the brand to terminate the deal.

However, what if you had already produced all the deliverables and were waiting for their final approval to publish them?

Should the brand be able to walk away, compensating you nothing?

No, that's not going to fly.

You must avoid language in the termination clause that allows the brand

"the right to terminate the contract for any or for no reason, in its sole discretion, upon X days' notice."

Instead, the termination clause must include something like,

"In the event of termination by Client, [You] shall be entitled to the pro rata portion of any compensation paid or payable up to the date of such termination."

I've even broken it down further on more complex deals that include many deliverables:

*"In the event of termination by Client, [You] shall be enti-
tled to the following compensation upon completion of the
following milestones:*

- *Approved concept & production greenlight: 25%*
- *Submitted deliverables & awaiting Client feedback: 75%*
- *Approved deliverables & awaiting publication: 100%"*

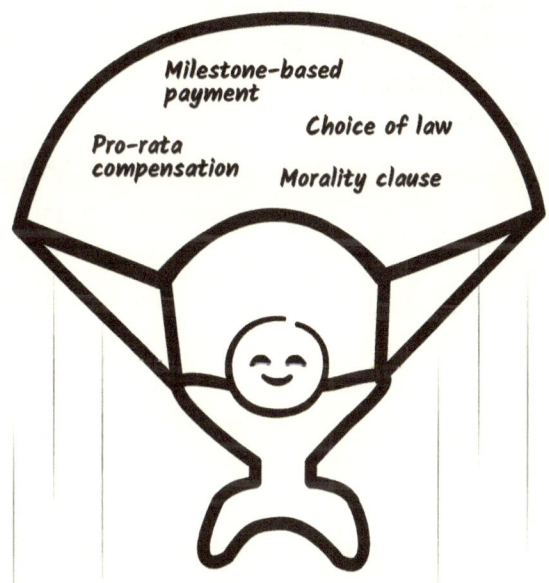

Additionally, there will usually be a section where the choice of
law or venue is outlined such as:

*"This Agreement shall be governed in all respects by the laws
of the State of Missouri and Influencer and Lender agree that
unless otherwise indicated by Agency any action arising from
or relating to this Agreement shall be brought exclusively in a
state or federal court located in St. Louis County, Missouri."*

Where it can get tricky is if the brand is located in a different country. If something happens and the brand breaches the contract, there's not much you can do. Sometimes, a foreign brand may be willing to agree during the negotiation to amend the venue to virtual arbitration via an international arbitral forum. The worst they can say is "no". Then you'll just need to decide if it's worth rolling the dice and proceeding with the deal.

One last termination consideration has to do with something called a "Morals" or "Morality" clause. Many brands are terrified of getting embroiled in a public relations crisis if they partner with a creator who is then caught saying or doing something morally reprehensible. The problem is brands love drafting these clauses quite broadly where if a creator has ever committed or commits any unlawful act the brand can terminate the contract. If interpreted literally, the brand could fire you, without pay, if they found out you drank one time underage or jaywalked. The Morals clause should always be limited to conduct that would negatively impact the brand's reputation.

Confirm the payment terms and method so you're not surprised.

One of the biggest gripes I've heard about the sponsorship process is that brands can sometimes take forever to pay.

But seeing as visiting the brand's headquarters wielding a crowbar with a cocked eyebrow isn't considered "acceptable" these days, it's critical you're crystal clear about the payment terms.

The common language you'll see is "Net 30," which means the brand or agency will remit payment thirty days after "completion of services" (after you finish or publish everything).

But more and more companies are listing Net 60 or even Net 90 on contracts.

I don't know about you, but that feels like a long time to wait to see a single dollar.

No, no. Put the crowbar down, remember?

It's perfectly reasonable to request 50% of the total compensation (at the brand's standard Net terms) upon *contract execution* and the remaining balance after the Completion of Services.

By the way, nothing is stopping you from asking for even more aggressive terms like Net 7 if the brand will go for it! The worst they can say is, "No."

Also, one universal truth I've learned after hundreds of sponsorships is that brands have wildly different processes for paying invoices.

Some prefer paying via ACH, some prefer sending a wire, and some might even ask for your PayPal details.

And yes, a few will insist on mailing you a paper check. Sigh.

Oh, don't forget the lengthy vendor and tax paperwork you'll have to fill out.

It's a losing battle to complain and ask why it's necessary or if they'll change their process.

Just grit your teeth, smile, fill out the forms, tell them the payment method works great, and move on.

Assume benevolence, not malevolence, when you find an error.

About 25% of the time, when I receive a sponsorship contract, there is some kind of material error or omission that doesn't align with what I believe was negotiated.

Instead of getting mad and assuming the brand is trying to mislead me intentionally, I calmly reply:

> *"Thanks so much for sending over the contract! Overall, it looks great! Just a few things I caught (see attached for my comments)."*

Remember, the brand or agency is probably working with 30 or 40 other partners, and since everyone has a slightly different SOW, it's far more likely their copy-and-paste skills suck.

The vast majority of the time, when I flag these discrepancies, the brand says, "Oops, sorry about that. Just updated it."

Trust me: the sponsorship process (and life) will be more pleasant when you assume people are nice, not evil.

So, we've arrived at the point where you have an airtight contract.

You sign it, and the brand countersigns...woohoo!

It's time to hit the ground running and start creating, right?

Not so fast.

Even if the brand says, "We're giving you 100% creative freedom..."

Never, ever, ever take them at their word.

100% of the time, you must put together a Concept (Step 4) for how you'll bring the partnership to life, which allows the brand to provide feedback and final buy-in on the creative vision.

Bonus:
Claim the free bonus from this chapter
at ***sponsormagnet.com/contract***
- Smart contract interpretation checklist

Concept

A few years after starting my influencer marketing agency I received a Request for Proposal (RFP) from a large toy brand.

They were doing a big re-brand and wanted to engage family-focused creators to spread awareness.

The best part? Their budget was eye-popping.

It was also squarely in my agency's wheelhouse, so I huddled with my team and devised a killer proposal.

A few weeks after submitting it, the brand asked us to fly out and present the strategy in person. Nerve-wracking, but we made the trip and I felt we knocked it out of the park.

Then came the waiting game.

The date the brand said they'd make a final decision came and went.

Each time we followed up, the brand said it wouldn't be much longer.

After six excruciating weeks, I got a call from a senior executive at the brand who told me we had won the deal!

Only one condition: we had to launch the campaign on the original proposed date, despite the six-week delay. Gulp.

"No problem!" I said.

Then, the reality of what I just agreed to sunk in.

On a very short timeline, we'd need to:
- Recruit, onboard, and sign contracts with 20 creators
- Ship every person specific toys, depending on their kids' ages
- Conduct calls to ensure the creators knew what to do
- Allow the creators 7-10 days for production and submission of initial drafts

It was possible but didn't leave much margin for error.

After signing the contract with the brand, I emailed them and asked if they could send a creative brief outlining the key talking points and call to action.

When they delivered it a few days later, the brand suggested having a call the following week to review the brief in detail. They also requested a few high-level ideas from each partner about their content direction. Ugh.

At this point, every day mattered if we wanted to hit the launch deadline and I was concerned these extra steps would come at the expense of time that *could* have been spent producing the assets.

I told the brand we could skip those things since the brief looked fantastic and we had confidence these particular creators would make something awesome.

To my surprise, the brand said, "OK."

Are you getting a bad feeling in your stomach that something terrible is about to happen?

If so, that's impressive, because I, like an idiot, did not!

I was proud of myself for keeping this project on track. The following two weeks were a blur. Liaising with the creators. Shipping out all the products and ensuring they were received. Organizing all the content as everyone began submitting.

Against all odds, my team successfully delivered all the draft content to the brand by the original promised date.

Before we even had a chance to high-five, the senior exec at the brand quickly emailed us back:

"Call me ASAP."

Never a message you want to receive.

Remember when I mentioned that we had shipped age-specific toys for each creator's kids?

Turns out that when a product has a minimum age rating (e.g., 3+), you cannot depict a kid younger than that in any promotional content.

Though we painstakingly ensured each creator had a kid in the proper age range, *we did not tell them* they couldn't include their other younger kids in the content (because we didn't know that was an issue).

The exec took one look and immediately rejected the content, even though the infants *weren't interacting with the products.*

I promised the exec we would figure out a solution and hung up.

What a nightmare.

While I briefly considered editing 37 babies out of the videos frame by frame using editing skills I did not have, I ultimately decided to pay the affected creators more money to reshoot their content without the younger kids. At the end of the day, this entire thing was my fault.

Had we scheduled the extra briefing call and submitted the creators' visions, we would have almost certainly caught this.

I learned two valuable lessons from that experience:

1. Even smart people can make stupid decisions (me, I'm talking about me).
2. Taking extra time with brands that might have specific legal or regulatory exposure is shrewd.

Now, if you think expectation misalignment is a problem only agencies run into...think again.

One of the top gripes I hear from the creators I coach is that brands love introducing new requirements halfway through production.

Or worse, brands voice bizarre concerns after everything is already produced.

The only way to avoid 99% of these issues is to submit a concept for the brand to review and provide feedback on *before you start production.*

"But Justinnnnnnn, that's so much worrrrrrk."

Stop. 100% of the time, send your concept.

No exceptions.

Common mistakes and pitfalls with concepts.

- Starting production when the brand says, "We trust you"
- Demonstrating or displaying the product or service incorrectly
- Not properly disclosing the partnership legally

Let's imagine an ideal world in which a brand contacts you and says it wants to pay you a lot of money for its next campaign.

They have a specific, well-articulated vision of how they want you to bring the partnership to life.

They tell you they want it to be "organic" and "authentic." They also defer to you *entirely* regarding the creative direction and strategy.

Sounds like a dream, right?

That's because it is. As in, it rarely happens.

Many brands don't know what they want (or want something unrealistic) and you must educate them on what information you'll need to ensure the partnership's success.

That information should be summarized into a "Creative Brief."

Request a succinct "Creative Brief" so everyone is on the same page.

A creative brief should be a simple 1-2 page document provided by a brand or agency that outlines everything you'll need to know to start production.

I say "should be" because many brands have never created a brief before or are skeptical of its necessity.

Some brands will even complain it will slow down the partnership process.

Resist the temptation to let them off the hook.

Creating a brief will force the brand to regroup internally and be more thoughtful about what they expect you to deliver.

The best briefs have four primary ingredients:
- Key messages or talking points (3-4 bullets max)
- Mood boards or visual brand guidelines
- One call-to-action (not multiple)
- DOs and DON'Ts section

Creative Brief Toolbox

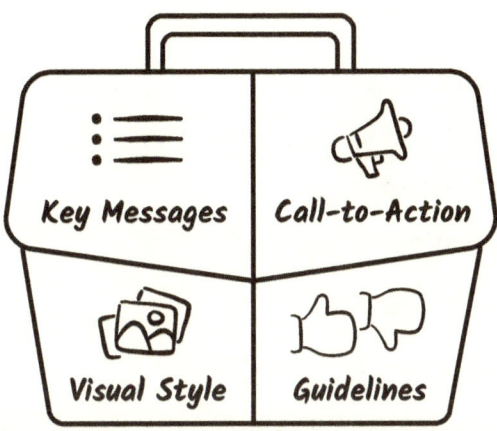

Key Messages

While many brands will be unfamiliar with briefs, others will be *too* familiar, stuffing them with 20 bullet points on the company's 200-year history plus 15-20 additional talking points.

It's your job to explain that robotically regurgitating irrelevant brand trivia to your audience will result in pushback.

Instead, ask them to highlight the 3-4 *most important* elements to include so your integration can be concise and potent.

This is especially important for in-person or virtual events where the sponsor will be integrated into the programming.

Mood boards or visual brand guidelines

Sometimes it's hard for brands to articulate the "vibe" they're going for with the partnership.

Requesting they provide example "mood board" imagery or videos will help you know right off the bat whether your creative direction will resonate.

Call-to-action (CTA)

It's tempting for brands to request you instruct your audience to do multiple things:

"Follow us on social media!"

"Download our whitepaper!"

"Scan this QR code to get 10% off!"

The problem with this is, when instructed to do multiple things, most people in your audience will do nothing. Heck, you probably got so tired trying to find a TV show to watch amongst 1,000 options that you gave up and started reading this book instead! Great choice, by the way.

Asking the brand to pick the *most critical* CTA they want you to make (which should almost always be tied to the primary campaign objective) will ensure your audience knows exactly what to do.

To make your case extra convincing, cite research by Wordstream that found emails with a single CTA (vs. multiple or none) increased clicks by 371%.

DOs and DON'Ts

Despite their best efforts, brands regularly omit critical details of what they expect you to do.

Thankfully, omissions can usually be added or fixed without much extra work.

However, the more dire situation is when brands forget to tell you things they *don't* want you to do.

Especially if you're not familiar with the brand, product, or service, it's easy to misrepresent something accidentally.

Ask the brand to clarify the following:

- *What's the proper way to pronounce the brand/ product name?*
  - Can you provide a phonetic spelling?
- *What's the appropriate way to showcase the product/service?*
  - This is especially important for tutorial or event partnerships
- *Can you share common questions or concerns you've gotten when other partners activated?*
  - This allows you to address these proactively
- *How would you like me to handle negative responses or comments related to the post or product online?*
  - Delete? Reply? Moderate?
- *Is there anything NOT covered in this brief that the brand is particularly sensitive about?*
  - When April and I asked one agency this, they said, "Please don't wear ripped jeans when filming. The brand hates that." (She was planning on wearing ripped jeans when she filmed the next day...GOOD TO KNOW).
- *Can you send published examples the brand loved from other partners?*

- This will give you an idea of what the brand has already approved

Here's an example of a DOs and DON'Ts section from a real Creative Brief we received:

Do:
- *Use language you would normally use on your own channels*
- *Focus on aspects of your personal life that fans will appreciate access to*
- *Stay positive and upbeat, and feel free to be yourself*
- *Let your personality shine through*
- *Share posts on [Partner/Advertiser] provided specific dates and times*

Don't:
- *Share posts outside of Advertiser approved posting hours*
- *In general, refrain from negative comments about Advertiser industry*
- *Feature alcohol or drugs or any other illegal activities or substances*
- *Be overly sarcastic, bordering on mean*
- *Feature competitor products, logos, or names in copy or creative*
- *Share any posts that aren't Advertiser-friendly in nature, risqué in any way, or include profanity*
- *Use third party regrams, drawings, GIFs and Memes*
- *Use trademarks not approved by Advertiser in content or copy (i.e. other brand names,*
- *movie titles, songs, etc.)*

- *Change Advertiser approved video, photo, or copy in any way, including adding filters or cropping content*
- *Engage or respond to negative fan comments*
- *Directly target children under the age of 18 within the Content*

The main takeaway should be that every brand has different sensitivities, and overlooking a single item could result in a reshoot, revision, or even termination of the partnership.

Proactively brainstorm objections your audience might have so you can address them.

Think of your behavior as a regular consumer for a second.

When you're deciding whether to buy a product in a retail store or online, you likely ask yourself all sorts of questions, such as:

"Will this solve my problem?"

"Will it be easy to set up?"

"Did this work for other people?"

"Can I find a better deal elsewhere?"

Your audience will undergo the same evaluation process when you publish your sponsorship, so you must proactively brainstorm what objections they might raise.

There are a few easy ways you can do this:

- Read reviews for the product or service. Are there common complaints or questions? Your audience is likely to have the same ones.
- Look through online forums where people are posting about issues they're having.
- Read through the comment sections on posts from past partners they hired.

Once you've identified a short list of potential objections, you can address them head-on in your concept.

Submit a thorough overview of exactly what you'll say, do, or show.

Even if the brand has not asked you to send them a concept of how you'll bring the partnership to life, you must do it every time.

Ideally, this would include a storyboard, a high-level script, or, at minimum, 2-3 sentences via email.

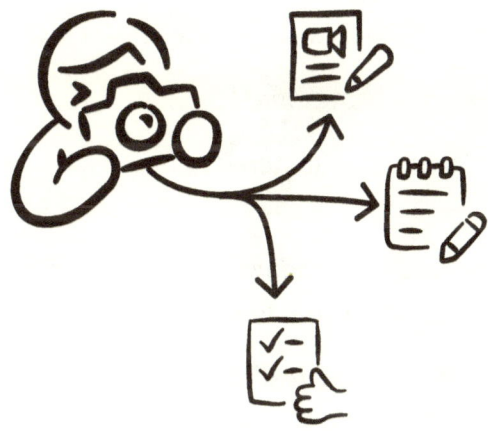

You have to send something that allows them a chance to say, *"Wait a minute. We were thinking you would do another thing entirely."*

Perfect. That's the type of feedback you want at this stage.

You can then communicate with the brand until you have a much better understanding of what they're expecting.

Here's an example of a script we wrote for a sponsorship with a brand we knew was extra cautious about how their products were depicted.

Wardrobe: Solid colors, loungewear, no labels/name brands.

Intro: Establishing shot of April and her two sons sitting on the sofa in the living room enjoying each other's company.

April's husband, Justin, comes on screen.

Justin: "Guys, look what I've got."

Justin temptingly holds up a package of [brand's product].

April: "Ooooh, can I have one?"

Justin says: "Well, we partnered with [Brand], so of course you can!"

Justin hands April the product. Close on April opening the product. Close on April, about to take a big bite.

Right when she sinks her teeth into [Brand's product], there's a sudden flash/transition, and the living room is transformed into a dance party!

The scenery will be decorated with the following items:
- *Metallic tinsel*
- *Disco decor*
- *Colorful lights*

We'll be suddenly wearing:
- *Metallic party hats*
- *LED light-up glasses*

Note: we will use the following royalty-free music tracks:
- *Track 1*

- *Track 2*

Our kids will be busting a move while Justin does the worm. Just a super fun-filled scene!

Then, suddenly, we'll cut back to the normal living room where April is "finishing" the bite of [Brand's product]. She'll look dazed, and Justin and the boys will look at her curiously.

April (to herself): "So fluffy."

April's son: "You OK, Mom?"

April: "Couldn't be better!"

Justin and the boys shrug it off and then grab their own [Brand's product].

Right before they bite in unison, April looks straight at the camera with a smirk.

April: "Here we go again!"

There are a few things you'll likely notice about this script:
- It's incredibly detailed, leaving nothing to chance
- We linked the exact supplies and music tracks we were planning to use

If you're thinking this seems like a ton of unnecessary effort or destroys your creativity (especially if they're not asking for a script), ask yourself what's better:

An extra thirty minutes of work upfront or an extra day at the end to revise/reshoot the whole thing?

Also, remember: not every sponsorship will require a detailed script.

Here's another concept example from a deal we did with a brand we knew was more easy-going:

April's followers *love* her "Clean With Me" videos, so she will do a "Deep Car Clean With Me."

She will highlight how no job is complete without [Brand's product]!

The visual style will be similar to her other cleaning videos, in which she shoots lots of "speed-cleaning" footage accompanied by a voiceover incorporating all the brief's talking points.

No other cleaning product labels will be shown.

In this example, we linked to past videos April had done in this vein so the brand knew the exact content style she was envisioning.

Here's an even simpler example from a newsletter integration I did:

I would love to highlight exceptional testimonials or case studies from other creators in the [Brand's partnership program].

This allowed the brand to give a thumbs-up or thumbs-down on the high-level creative direction I was planning.

There are a few more critical things to confirm with the brand when you submit your concept.

Confirm the who, what, where, and when.

 **WHO**    **WHAT**    **WHERE**    **WHEN**

Who will be included?

When a brand signs a sponsorship contract with you, they expect you to be the only person involved in bringing the work to life.

So imagine their surprise when you turn in a video featuring your partner who has a tattoo of a copyrighted cartoon character.

Uh-oh.

Or maybe you decide to film in public, only for the brand to ask if you got signed "releases" from all the people in the background, permitting you to include their names and likenesses.

Yikes.

Or maybe you enlist the help of a new ghostwriter to write a sponsored blog post. The brand then reposts the article on its website and is later sued by your ghostwriter for copyright infringement. Only then do you realize you didn't have an owner-ship clause in your contract with your ghostwriter.

Oops.

Believe me when I say it's always better to be upfront with the brand about who will be a part of your production.

What are you submitting?

Does the brand need a specific word count?

Do they need it shot in 4K resolution?

Do you have to capture still photos as well as video footage?

Should videos be shot in landscape or portrait orientation?

After production has wrapped, it's hard to go back and recreate assets you forgot.

Where will you produce it?

If you're producing a video, are you shooting in your family room? If so, do you have clearance for the painting on your wall? If not, remove it before shooting.

If you're producing an event, where will the brand's signage go?

When will you submit it?

There's nothing worse than receiving a frantic message from the brand asking why you haven't submitted anything or completed the project yet.

Brands often have little understanding of how long it takes to produce solid work, so well ahead of time, pick a submission date and don't miss it.

Now, let's assume the brand emails you with great news:

> *"Your concept looks awesome and you have the green light to move forward with production!"*

Time to put your head down, put your phone on "Do Not Disturb," ignore your email inbox for a week, and crank everything out, right?

Not so fast.

Your professionalism and attention to detail during Step 5 (Produce) often determine whether a brand hires you again...or not.

Bonus:

Claim the free bonus from this chapter
at ***sponsormagnet.com/concept***

- Creative brief breakdown checklist

Produce

Several years ago, April and I secured a last-minute sponsorship with a large home fragrance brand.

They were launching a new program where you could recycle used fragrance cartridges at major retailers and get a discount on a new cartridge.

They needed the content posted that week, so we promised to produce it over the weekend and deliver the draft assets for approval on Monday morning.

Saturday turned out to be very busy, so we woke up bright and early Sunday morning, ready to shoot for the brand.

When we arrived at our local retailer, we couldn't find the brand's special recycling "end cap" anywhere. We asked several employees and even the store manager about it, and they had no idea what we were talking about.

Not good.

Maybe this location just didn't have it yet?

We decided to try another location about 20 minutes away.

No luck.

Then we tried another location, even further away.

Nothing.

At this point, we'd wasted about three hours driving all over with nothing to show for it.

We had no choice but to contact our agency representative to find out what to do.

Thankfully, our contact's cell phone number was listed in her email signature, and when we called, she picked up!

We explained the whole situation, and she was equally perplexed.

Unfortunately, she couldn't contact the brand until the next day to determine which locations had the special display.

At this point, most creators would point their finger at the brand or agency.

"They should have known. Ugh. They completely wasted my time!"

In reality, this was *our fault*. Poor planning.

We should have never assumed that every retailer nation-wide had the unique display (we later learned only a small fraction did).

Confirming beforehand that you have everything you need to complete your job is vital to the production process.

This means:

- If you're picking up the item at a store, ask for the exact location, exact SKU (Stock-Keeping Unit), or exact image/URL of what you're supposed to get or show
- If the brand is mailing the item to you, ask for expedited delivery and tracking info
- If the brand is providing you with access to a product (e.g., software, service, app, etc.), ensure you have the proper credentials, permissions, and lead time to evaluate it

With the fragrance brand sponsorship, we ultimately had to drive quite a distance to a completely different retailer several days later.

When the partnership was finally published, it was significantly past the date the brand initially requested.

Regardless of whose fault it was (or whether it was fair)...

Because we didn't deliver the content when we said we would, *we never got another sponsorship from that brand.*

We ultimately learned that such situations can be avoided by having a meticulously planned production process.

Common mistakes and pitfalls during production.

- Realizing the day before it's due that you're missing info or don't have the right product
- Making the brand's life difficult by not keeping them updated
- Turning drafts in late, in a super disorganized manner, or with something missing

There's a simple thing you can add to your production process that will separate you from other partners: proactive communication.

When you encounter roadblocks that might affect your timeline or work quality, let the brand or agency know.

This will allow them time to remediate the situation and, more critically, communicate with their boss or client to level-set expectations.

The worst thing you can do is go rogue and start making executive decisions about how to proceed, given the new conditions or project dynamics.

Stick to the approved concept and don't deviate.

One of the most frustrating parts of running my influencer marketing agency was receiving draft content back from partners that was completely different from the concept the brand had approved.

When I'd politely ask about the discrepancy (while I died inside), the responses always floored me:

"I just thought it sounded better this way."

"When I started filming, I realized it wouldn't work."

"The brand should trust me because I know my audience best."

While all those things might be true, the brand must approve any changes beforehand.

What many creators don't realize is that there are often a ton of people inside organizations who have to sign off on your concept, such as:

- Managers
- Directors
- Vice Presidents
- Legal Affairs & Compliance
- Public Relations
- Partner Agencies

Even though you might think how you describe a product or service is harmless, brands often have strict guidelines and standards all external partners must adhere to.

Remember the toy brand that couldn't feature kids below a certain age in ads?

That's because they get sued all the time by parents whose kids were injured while using the toys. I guess it makes sense, since kids and self-preservation mix about as well as oil and water.

The last thing you want to do is put your contact in a tricky spot where they must explain why you deviated from the approved plan to their boss or client.

If you genuinely feel midway through production that a change must be made, *always always always* clear it with the brand or agency before proceeding.

Accommodate all mid-production requests, with a few exceptions.

One time April and I were in the middle of production for a sponsorship with a jewelry brand and our contact emailed us with a frantic message:

> *"We unexpectedly ran out of stock on the item you're promoting."*

Talk about a nightmare scenario for the brand.

They just committed to paying us a lot of money, and if we published that content, no one could buy anything.

Instead of crossing our arms and saying, "That's too bad, not our problem..." (which many creators do!), we offered two possible solutions:

- Change our Call-to-Action to encourage our audience to join a waitlist for the item
- Keep the asset as-is and wait to publish until the stock is replenished

The brand chose the first option, and we re-recorded a simple voiceover at the end of the integration to modify our CTA.

Rather than getting upset at a brand when unexpected things happen, it's critical to have empathy.

In almost all situations, they're not purposefully introducing new requirements just to mess with you.

Instead, if your default response becomes, "No worries, I got you!" you will quickly develop a reputation as someone brands want to hire repeatedly.

To be clear, brands will sometimes ask for annoying or unnecessary things that are objectively unreasonable.

Which is why you're totally within your rights to calmly explain why you can't accommodate these requests if they're outside the scope of the current partnership.

Usually, the brand will back off.

But if they don't, start a dialogue about the incremental compensation required to make it happen.

Disclose your relationship with the brand, no exceptions.

There are two groups of people to never upset: your audience and your government.

The easiest way to anger your audience (and destroy your credibility) is to not disclose when a brand or company has provided you something of value in exchange for promotion.

And FYI, "something of value" also means free products or affiliate commission, not just flat compensation!

This is more than just a high-integrity business practice. It's the *law*.

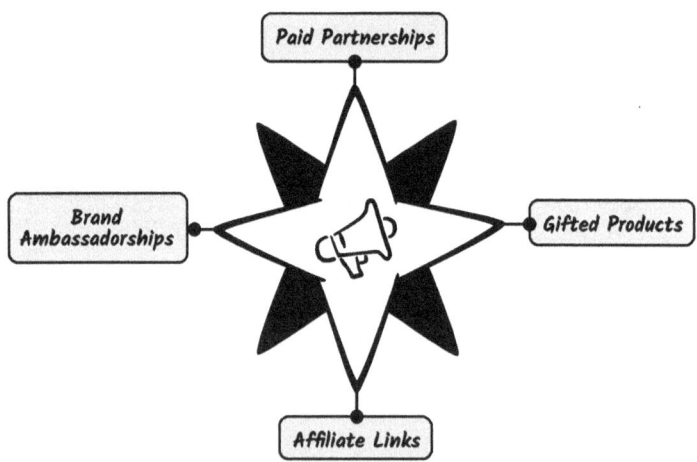

In the United States, for example, there is a governing body called the Federal Trade Commission (FTC) that enforces civil antitrust law and promotes consumer protection.

The FTC legally mandates that you disclose your brand relation-ships to ensure your audience isn't duped by misleading or false advertising practices.

And while I know you'd never dream of misleading your audience (right?!), there will inevitably be some brands who overtly ask you to remove your sponsorship disclosures.

They may try to argue that the chances of getting caught are slim, but the FTC and other global regulatory bodies have started handing out fines to brands and creators who fail to comply.

I'm not making any of this up, by the way.

You might find this hard to believe, but here's an actual reply we got from a brand when we submitted draft content for review:

> *"Can you leave out the '#ad' since that will decrease the traffic?"*

Sneaky, sneaky.

We immediately responded:

> *"To comply with FTC disclosure guidelines, we need to have either #ad or #sponsored in the caption. Let us know which you'd prefer."*

The brand relented.

Whether they were ignorant of the law or purposefully disregard-ing it, it's your job to educate them and be firm in your stance.

> *"But Justin, do I **really** have to disclose every single time?!"*

I understand there's sometimes nuance, so let's go through a few scenarios, shall we?

What if the brand gives you a free product in exchange for a review?

Yes. You must tell your audience the item was gifted.

What about if a brand pays you money for a post?

Yes. Most people get that one.

What about a free trip somewhere or a hotel stay?

Yes. That's something of value.

What about other VIP perks? Maybe you purchased tickets to an event and then connected with the PR manager, who upgraded your tickets to even better ones.

Depends. If the requirement for that upgrade was that you'd promote the event, you'll have to disclose that perk was gifted.

I constantly receive emails and direct messages from people describing esoteric partnerships, asking whether or not they need to disclose.

My rule of thumb is just to do it.

There is little downside. A few vocal audience members may get annoyed, but in the end, who cares? You're displaying your integrity and, on the off-chance your government ever starts sniffing around, you're covered.

So, *how* should you adequately disclose a partnership?

Every regulatory body is different, but, in general:
- Place the disclosure where it's impossible to miss
- Don't bury or mix the disclosure into a group of hashtags/links
- Use simple language like "Thanks to ACME for sponsoring this video" or "Thanks to ACME for sending the free wine fridge." (Yes, I got a free wine fridge. Yes, I'm bragging about it.)

- For text-based disclosures, you're usually fine using #gifted, #affiliate, #ad, or #sponsored. Don't use weird, confusing ones like #sp #spon #collab. Also, saying you're "working with" the brand isn't clear because your average audience member won't understand what that means.

When in doubt, just be transparent, honest, and direct about your relationship with a sponsor.

Balance your "infomercial" concerns with pragmatism.

You don't have to do too many sponsorships before noticing your audience's response to them can be...fickle.

Less engagement. Less views. More snark.

Whether consciously or subconsciously, many creators begin producing work that mentions or features the product as briefly as they can get away with.

But put yourself in the brand's shoes. Maybe they're paying you $1,000 for a short-form video or $100,000 to be the presenting sponsor of your event.

It's reasonable for them to expect you'll give their product adequate "airtime."

By over-indexing on your audience's satisfaction, you run the risk of fracturing your relationship with your sponsor.

Now, I'm not saying you need to transform into a late-night "infomercial" host, but it's critical to remember why the brand hired you.

While some of your sponsored work may underperform, it will also allow you to reinvest back into your business. Maybe pay your rent or mortgage? Pay for a trip to the tropics? Is that such a bad thing?

As with everything, it's a balancing act.

Just don't forget to be pragmatic.

Organize your drafts so there's minimal back-and-forth.

I'll never forget one creator I hired through my agency who was supposed to deliver 15 pictures for the brand to approve that she'd be posting over the next few months.

When we followed up with her about when she'd be able to submit, we received *15 separate emails,* each with a single photo attached.

"*But surely the pictures were titled in such a way that it was clear which ones were which, right Justin?*"

Oh, my sweet summer child.

It didn't end there.

We started receiving *more* emails from the creator, each with different captions they planned to use.

Did the creator indicate which captions were supposed to go with which picture?

Hah. Hahaha. Hahahahahahaha.

Multiply this chaos by 20 partners and you can see how much extra work sloppy submission practices adds to the plate of your contact.

Instead, be a professional.

Create a comprehensive submission document that outlines all your deliverables clearly.

For example, if you're doing a podcast sponsorship, include precisely what you'll add to the show notes like:

- CTA (Call-to-action), e.g., "Click here to find out where to purchase!"
- FTC disclosures like #ad, #sponsored, or "Thanks to ACME for sponsoring me!"
- Any campaign hashtags the brand requests, e.g., #ACMErocks
- Proposed title: [Will you include the brand/product name in the title?]
- Podcast thumbnail: [Will you include the brand/product logo in the cover art?]

Every platform will have unique publication characteristics, so it's your job to proactively highlight things like the caption, associated text, or links you plan on using.

Also, verify whether the brand wants to preview the *entire* asset or just the ad read.

One time, April and I landed a sponsorship with a cleaning brand and we only sent them the two-minute integration that talked about their product.

"Looks great!" they said.

We then inserted that ad toward the front end of a longer 15-minute "Clean With Me" video and published it.

The brand freaked out because they felt another product April had used was "competitive."

No, that wasn't in the agreement. And no, they never mentioned that previously.

But it still put us in a tricky spot.

The brand ultimately calmed down and agreed it wasn't a huge deal, but it quickly could have escalated.

It's on *you* to get the brand's buy-in for every tiny detail so there are no surprises.

Submit your drafts when you say you will.

Here's a depressing stat.

When I ran my influencer marketing agency, only 50% of creators turned their draft content in on time.

50%! This is across hundreds of campaigns we ran over the years.

Initially, I thought we sucked at finding partners that took these engagements seriously, but even as our vetting criteria grew more stringent the average barely budged.

So we began creating internal "ghost" timelines that required the creators to submit their drafts 5-7 days before the delivery date we had committed to the brand. This allowed us much-needed slippage to chase all the stragglers down and ensure we could submit everything in one big "package."

The last thing our clients wanted was for us to submit everything piecemeal.

"Here's this creator's content."

"Oh, here's another."

"Can you approve this one now?"

What's the point of the brand hiring our agency, then? One of our core value propositions was that we would streamline the collaboration process with partners (and this was not that).

So even if five of the 10 creators we hired turned their drafts in on time, we still had to wait until we collected the remaining partners' content before submitting everything to the brand.

If you've ever wondered why it sometimes takes agencies weeks to get back to you with feedback from the brand, this is often one of the reasons.

The late delivery problem got so bad that my agency eventually developed a short list of creators we knew always submitted their drafts on time.

When we were recruiting for new campaigns, if there were even a *remote* chance those reliable creators could be a fit, we'd prioritize them in our recommendations.

Remember, the bar is low. It's in the basement, actually.

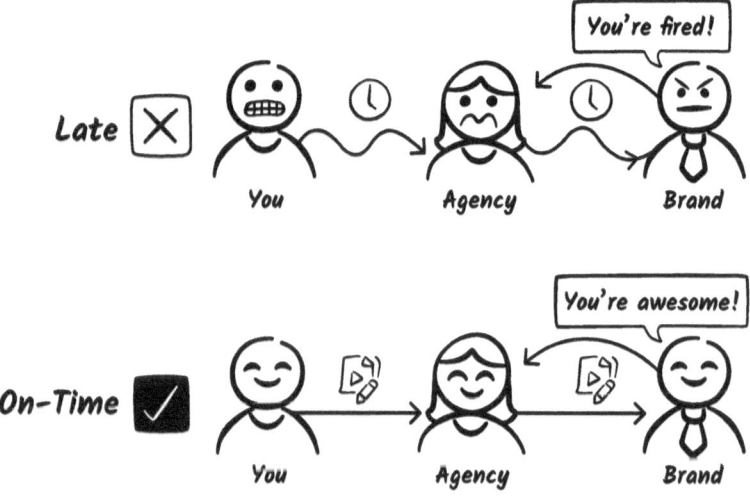

If you turn your drafts in when you say you will, you'll be way ahead.

Now, we've arrived at one of the most frustrating aspects of sponsorships:

Submitting work for review (that you think is great!) only for the brand or agency to tell you it sucks.

Well, they usually won't outright say it sucks, but they'll send you a zillion "suggestions" for how you should revise it to make it "better."

Let's discuss how to appropriately respond to Feedback (Step 6) so that your relationship with the brand is reinforced, not soured.

Bonus:

Claim the free bonus from this chapter
at *sponsormagnet.com/produce*

- Sponsorship Draft Submission Template

Feedback

One summer, April and I inked a sponsorship with a consumer health brand that wanted to show how effective their product was for families to treat minor wounds.

Because the brand was large and traditional, we purposefully came up with a simple concept:

There's nothing better than an outdoor picnic with the family. Especially when the local park has lots of space for our boys to run around and have fun!

But sometimes our active kids get a little *too* active and have little accidents!

We'd love to capture a picnic scene in which the first photo shows us applying the product to one of our kids' knees.

The second photo will be a close-up shot showing a zoomed-in view of the product against the picnic backdrop.

In the caption, we'll share that the product has always helped us stay prepared as a family.

The brand's agency quickly approved our concept with minimal feedback and we got to work planning a picnic day at the park with our boys.

I bought a red and white checkered blanket, a wicker picnic basket, and a bunch of snacks from the grocery store.

We got to the park and started setting everything up.

I arranged snacks around the product for the second photo from our concept ("Close-up shot showing a zoomed-in view against the picnic backdrop").

I'm no production designer, but I thought it looked pretty cool.

We finished taking all the photos, had a great rest of the day at the park, cleaned up, and went home.

After submitting all the drafts to the agency, the waiting game began for feedback.

We steeled ourselves for a long wait (typical for a huge company), but after over a month, we grew concerned.

When we followed up, the agency said the brand had raised some issues, but they'd need a few more days.

Not good.

When the agency finally got back to us, here's what they said:

> *"The brand shared they'd like to limit the proximity of food to their products for all content pieces moving forward."*

Not only was this "avoid food" requirement never mentioned in the creative brief, but our concept (approved by the brand!) was centered around a *picnic.* Come on.

Was the agency seriously asking us to go back to the park, set everything up again, and re-shoot all the assets?

Oh, and in case you were wondering, they were *not* offering to pay us more.

We were in a tricky spot because, per the language in the agreement, we could have dug our heels in and demanded additional compensation.

But other than this hiccup, everything was going so well with the brand and agency that the last thing we wanted to do was make a big fuss. So we racked our brains for other solutions.

I went back and reviewed the pictures again. Since the assets they had issues with were close-ups of the product, you couldn't tell where the photos were taken. There wasn't even any grass in the shots.

So I went into the garage, grabbed the picnic basket, blanket, and leftover product, then dragged everything into my backyard.

I laid the blanket down, positioned the picnic basket and product in the same orientation as the first draft, and snapped new photos.

They were nearly identical, minus the food!

I submitted the new assets shortly after, and the brand was thrilled!

Not only did we avoid a contentious situation, but the agency praised our resourcefulness.

It's human nature to become defensive when receiving feedback, especially if it's anything less than "you're amazing!"

But rather than directing your outrage toward the brand, ask yourself: "Is there a way I can do what they're asking in less than 30 minutes?"

Sure, it's annoying.

Sure, they technically should pay you more money for it.

But the reputation you'll gain as a flexible partner will be worth far more than a few more extracted dollars.

Common mistakes and pitfalls when receiving feedback.

- Asking for more money each time the brand requests edits
- Being snarky to the brand when they ask for revisions
- Not asking the brand deeper questions about WHY they want specific revisions
- Making your contact look bad by flat-out refusing

Almost everyone takes feedback from brands personally.

But it's not personal.

The brand is not sending notes asking you to revise or redo things simply because they want to make you mad or violate your creative genius.

It's because internal and external stakeholders have differing opinions about how your work (which they're paying you for) should ultimately appear/sound.

Also, your contact is often just the messenger, so directing your ire at them accomplishes little.

I take that back. The one thing it does accomplish is ensure they'll never hire you again.

Instead, you must understand *why* the brand or agency is requesting these changes.

Ask for detailed reasoning behind each piece of feedback.

When I first start working with clients and students, I learned many tend to treat brand feedback as gospel, especially if they haven't done a ton of sponsorships.

They feel they're not "allowed" to push back on any revision requests.

However, I remind them that just because a brand sends you feedback doesn't mean it's right.

Aren't you the one who has your finger on the pulse of what is and isn't working in your niche, industry, or platform?

The brand doesn't.

Sometimes, you must dig deep and find the confidence to tell a brand they're wrong (tactfully).

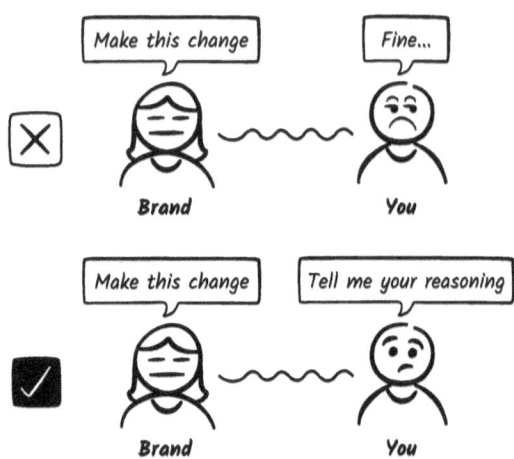

If you can provide a well-reasoned justification for why you shouldn't change what they're asking you to, they'll likely thank you!

I can't tell you how many brands have told April and me over the years, *"Wow, we didn't know about [insert best practice]. You're good to leave it as-is."*

Many people think that brands are the ultimate experts and have everything figured out, but that's not always the case.

Remember, don't just be a creator, influencer, or entrepreneur.

Be a *consultant*.

When to charge more money and when to do it for free.

Here's a simple framework:

Do it for free if...

- You agreed to X rounds of revisions in the contract (duh!)
- You didn't follow the approved concept or brief (take the L)
- It won't take you very long (stop whining if it'll take you five minutes to redo)
- There's a high chance of repeat business from a brand or agency (duh!)
- You'll make your contact a hero (Imagine the joy when they run to their boss or client and say, "Justin's amazing! He made the change for us even though he wasn't required to!")

Charge more money if...

- The brand is *well* past the contractual number of revisions
- The brand wants extensive revisions for things *not* included in the approved concept or brief
- Revising will take you the same amount of time (or longer) as the first production
- There's a *low* chance of repeat business (e.g., influencer marketing platform)

Your goal is to strike a balance between "doormat that agrees to every revision request" and "divo/diva that asks for thousands to change a five-second voiceover."

Why is feedback from brands so...stupid?

Here's real (hilarious) feedback we've received from brands:
- *"Can you reshoot this with a different color shirt?"*
- *"You didn't synchronize your dance moves enough."*
- *"I know we said we wanted you to write this in your 'voice,' but we changed our mind."*

Why do brands pull this stuff?

I want you to put on your empathy "hat" again (as heavy as it might feel by now).

Imagine you're a podcaster and hired a consultant to help promote your podcast.

You've spent years growing this podcast and have a profound connection with your audience.

You're also very sensitive about creative decisions related to your podcast.

So what would you do if that consultant created a promo that felt "off"?

You might not ask them to redo the whole thing, but you would likely ask for some tweaks.

Instead of a podcast, imagine you worked for a large brand with many different departments, each run by different managers with different motivations.

Every time you hire an external partner to promote your brand in any way, you must collect feedback from your boss, the VP of Marketing, the legal team, the public relations agency, and the paid media team.

There are corporate brand standards to uphold, you're reminded. The messaging has to be extremely precise because the last time you partnered with someone influential they said something inaccurate, and your customer service lines were overwhelmed. Oh, don't forget the legal exposure. Can't get sued. Your boss fails to tell you that this campaign needs to be finished in the next five days. You don't want to lose your job! You're hoping to get promoted this year and get a raise. So you ask the partner if they can submit the revisions within 24 hours so you can be a "hero" internally.

Whether right or wrong, stupid feedback is usually the result of dysfunctional company dynamics like this. It has nothing to do with you.

So suck it up and make the stupid revisions (they're paying you good money, after all)!

By the way, it's not just the brand's job to send *you* feedback.

It's *your job* to send the brand feedback if you think part of their conversion funnel is broken.

Send feedback to the brand so you see better results.

One time I inked a newsletter sponsorship with a financial services company, and when they sent me the landing page link they wanted me to direct my audience to, I immediately knew we had a problem.

The landing page didn't articulate the tool's value proposition well, the offer was confusing, and most importantly, nothing signified that my audience was in the right place.

Instead, I told the brand I'd love to create a unique video asset (which I was not contractually obligated to do) to explain in more detail why I loved the tool.

We'd include this video above the scroll, including a large headline, "Why Justin Moore loves [Brand's product]."

I also suggested we change the copy on the button to clarify the offer.

I explained that all these things would pull my audience further down the purchase funnel.

The brand was floored.

Not only had no one ever given them that level of feedback before, but they couldn't believe I was willing to do additional work to ensure the campaign's success.

But why wouldn't I?

It's in my best interest to do everything possible to drive more conversions, which will increase the chances the brand will hire me again!

"But Justin, I'm not a copywriter or user experience expert. What if the brand thinks my suggestions are dumb?"

You don't need to be an expert and they won't think you're dumb.

Just pretend you're one of your average audience members.

If you clicked on the sponsor's link, would it make sense to you? What is confusing?

What would make you immediately want to sign up or purchase it?

A big part of becoming a Sponsor Magnet is rewiring your preconceived notions of what's "normal" when collaborating with brands.

Screw what's normal.

Strive to be abnormal.

By the way, you know what's abnormal?

Partners who Publish their work correctly and on time (Step 7).

Bonus:
Claim the free bonus from this chapter
at *sponsormagnet.com/feedback*
- Handling Complex Feedback checklist

Publish

One of the worst mistakes April and I ever made early on came after we hit publish on a sponsored post for a large vitamin brand.

The deal was pretty typical up to that point. The pitch went smoothly, the negotiation was friendly, the concept was approved quickly, and there was minimal feedback on the asset we produced.

The brand asked when we could go live and we said as early as Saturday. We got the green light.

So, we woke up bright and early, uploaded the assets, copied and pasted the pre-approved caption, then added the tracking link and discount code they had provided—boom, published.

Almost immediately, comments flooded in saying that the discount code wasn't working.

My heart sank.

I stupidly assumed the brand had ensured the code was good to go!

I pulled up the website, entered the discount code, and, sure enough, got an "invalid promo" error message. Tried all caps, nope. All lowercase? No dice. Ugh.

I frantically emailed our brand contact, but it was Saturday! I didn't get a reply and couldn't find a phone number either.

(Note to self: stop doing stuff on weekends when brands are unreachable)

Meanwhile, hundreds of frustrated comments continued rolling in, and we could only apologize.

When we finally heard back from the brand on Monday, they quickly fixed the discount code, but it was too late.

All the momentum and interest from our audience had passed. We tried replying to as many comments as possible, letting people know the code was now working, but we had very few takers. We shuddered to think of all the people who tried to redeem the offer initially but got frustrated and didn't even leave a comment.

Do you think the vitamin brand ever worked with us again?

No. No, they didn't. The campaign was unprofitable, after all.

Most people blame the brand in these situations: "What kind of messed up operation are they running over there?!"

However, it's *your job* to verify crucial things (like the discount code) are working.

Why? If something doesn't work when you hit publish, your audience will likely get mad at *you,* not the brand.

Common mistakes and pitfalls when publishing.

- Not verifying the discount codes are valid & working
- Using the wrong handles/hashtags/tracking links
- Publishing work that hasn't been approved
- Publishing the wrong version of an asset
- Being unreachable after posting

Hundreds of people have now taken my free Sponsorship Wheel Snapshot (sponsormagnet.com/snapshot) and the data is clear: everyone rates themselves the highest on the Publish step.

This confidence makes sense. Publishing is what we do day in, day out as creators. It's how we've built our businesses from the ground up.

The problem is that many people are *too confident* to the point where they are sloppy and unprofessional.

The good news is I've got a handy publication checklist for you, so you're always organized and professional.

Create a checklist of everything you need before publishing.

Every time you're about to publish an asset or execute a sponsorship, ask yourself the following:

- *Am I using the final approved assets/copy?*
  - *Do NOT make any changes whatsoever that the brand hasn't approved.*

- *Am I including the correct brand handles, hashtags, and proper links, if applicable?*
  - *Tagging the wrong handle is common since brands often have different spellings across different platforms.*
- *Did I verify the discount code or offer is valid, if applicable?*
  - *Is the code case-sensitive?*
- *Is the product or service you're promoting out of stock or unavailable?*
  - *If so, do NOT publish the asset until you confirm the best action with the brand.*
- *Am I selecting the proper publication settings (audience visibility, paid partnership disclosure tools, etc.)?*
  - *Not disclosing the partnership properly can result in a breach of contract and/or audience blowback.*
- *Am I granting the brand the proper usage rights, if applicable?*
  - *Every platform has a different process to allow brands to run ads with your assets.*

If everything checks out, you should be good to hit publish!

Now it's time to kick your feet up, put your phone on Do Not Disturb, and go to the beach for the entire day, right?

No, please don't do that.

Don't hit publish, then be impossible to reach.

When I ran my agency, 30% of the time, when a creator would publish their sponsorship, we would catch some sort of error.

Sometimes, they used the wrong copy in the caption.

Sometimes, they mistyped the discount code.

Sometimes, the dang tracking link wasn't clickable.

You name it, I've seen it.

And because we often didn't know precisely when the creator would publish on a given day, we started monitoring their accounts like hawks to quickly flag any issues we caught.

The absolute worst was when we'd email someone within a few minutes of them publishing, calling out a problem, and we wouldn't hear from them for 6-8 hours...or even 1-2 days!

Meanwhile, their audience would leave tons of frustrated comments since they couldn't redeem the offer.

"Start an agency!" they said. "It'll be fun!" they said.

Narrator: it was not fun.

That reminds me: you've got another duty that will make the brand love you (even though you're not contractually obligated to do it).

Engage with your audience after publication.

When brands invest money into influencer marketing, especially if they haven't done many partnerships, they will be *very* excited for your sponsorship to go live.

And if you post on social media, the brand will refresh your comment section the moment you publish to see what people say about them.

The mistake many creators make is not responding or engaging with early comments at all.

This can frustrate the brand, especially if there are simple questions to answer but it would seem weird for the brand to jump in and reply.

Even though you might not think this sponsorship has high stakes, it might for the brand, so I encourage you to recalibrate how seriously you take it.

Collect early wins and send them to the brand.

When content is published on social media platforms that offer public-facing metrics (views, impressions, comments, etc.), it's easy for the brand to monitor the performance of a sponsorship.

But it's harder for brands to know how something is doing when performance metrics are not public or less obvious.

For example, if you're doing a newsletter sponsorship, the brand isn't seeing the replies you're getting to the email blast.

Or maybe you have event sponsors. They're only seeing how many people cruised through their booth.

You can fix that by screenshotting the heck out of early positive engagement you're receiving privately and sending that to the brand!

They are desperate for any indication, even anecdotal, that they made a good decision by hiring you for this sponsorship.

Here's an example of a text message I sent to the Partnerships Manager at community platform Circle after I published a sponsored video with them:

As you can see, positive comments like this get instantly shared internally *and* make your contact look like a genius.

And you can bet your booty they'll want to hire you again.

Proactively submit the published links and paperwork so you get paid quickly.

One thing that should be clear by now is that your brand contact is often overwhelmed and frustrated when dealing with unprofessional partners.

So, when a sponsorship is completed, make finalizing the campaign with you a breeze.

Send them links to all your published assets.

Send them the vendor paperwork they asked you to complete.

Send them your tax paperwork.

Send them your invoice with the Purchase Order (PO) number and payment terms correctly indicated.

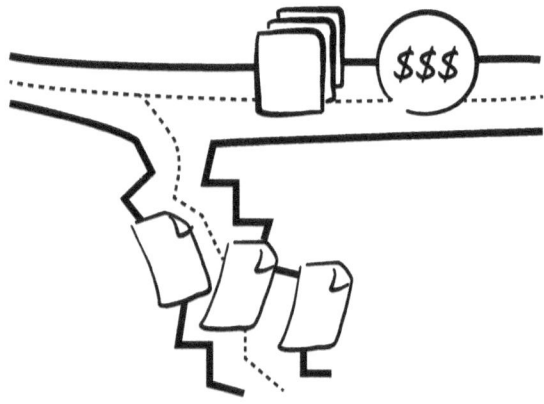

When I ran the agency, about 50% of the time we had to chase people down for missing documents, preventing us from closing the deal.

I'll never forget one creator we chased for three months because she was too busy to send us her invoice.

I guess she didn't need or want the thousands of dollars we were trying to send her (we finally paid her after four months...gee-whiz)!

Plcase, don't be that person.

Ask the brand for a testimonial and their reporting timeline.

When you've just published your sponsorship and submitted all the final paperwork, chances are the brand is at peak happiness.

You've been a joy to work with, they loved the assets you produced, and your professionalism is on full display.

Now is the time to ask the brand for a glowing testimonial!

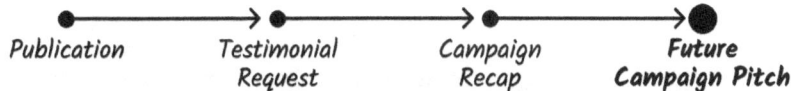

Publication   Testimonial   Campaign   *Future*
           Request   Recap   *Campaign Pitch*

Simply send them the following message:

> *"Thank you so much again for this amazing partnership! Out of curiosity, could you share a sentence or two about your experience working with me that I could include in my media kit?"*

Nine times out of 10, the brand will be happy to do it.

Here are a few testimonials April and I have received:

> *"April and Justin were fast to respond, an extreme pleasure to interact with, and it's the type of partnership you're hoping lands in your inbox so everyone can get their jobs done and get back to the pile of laundry waiting to be folded at home."*

> *"Our experience working with Justin and April has been great! They are incredibly timely with their responses, flexible and accommodating, and they met all deadlines for our campaign with them. We loved their work and are excited to work with them again in the near future."*

"Justin and April were an absolute dream to work with. From our initial outreach, we were blown away after receiving a personally recorded video expressing their interest and enthusiasm for this campaign. Throughout the campaign, they were prompt (and even early) on all deadlines, and all content was completely STELLAR and right on brief. We work with hundreds of creators each year, and we can confidently say that April and Justin were some of the best creators we've ever had the pleasure of working with. 10/10 recommend."

As a heads up, one out of 10 times that you ask for a testimonial, the brand will say no.

It's likely not because they're unhappy with your work but because their Public Relations team or client can't do it for fear of legal exposure.

Now it's finally time to go to the beach and chill, right?

I almost hear you muttering, *"Justin, let me put my dang phone on 'do not disturb' already!"*

Not quite yet. Take that bathing suit off. Actually, wait, don't. That sounded weird.

You must ask your contact when they plan on submitting a campaign recap to their boss or client.

Once you have that information, it's time to put together your *own* Post-Campaign Report that will blow the brand's socks off and make them want to hire you again (Step 8).

Bonus:
Claim the free bonuses from this chapter
at **sponsormagnet.com/publish**
- Publication prep checklist
- Testimonial request template

STEP 8

Analyze

Nathan Barry, CEO of email marketing platform Kit (formerly ConvertKit), revealed something surprising when I was on his podcast:

> "If we did a sponsored deal with a creator and they came back and said, 'Here's how it went, here's how it performed against your goals, here's all the feedback, here's the word on the street of what everyone is saying like, "I was thinking about using [Kit] once, but then I decided it was too much work to switch from Mailchimp so I never did it again."'

> "If the creator comes back and says, 'I did all this stuff and learned these ten things about your market,' we would say, 'This is amazing. Let's work with you more.' Even if the ROI wasn't quite where we wanted it from our initial forecast, if they come back with market insights and real feedback, then it's like, 'Great, let's tweak these things and go back into the market again with another campaign.'"

The lesson here is that conducting your own analysis, including quantitative and qualitative insights, will often lead to a new (or ongoing) sponsorship, ***even if the initial campaign underperformed.***

>"*But Justin, the brand only asked me to send screenshots of my insights or analytics.*"

Fine, do the bare minimum if you want to be like every other partner the brand hires.

But remember, since you tied your pitch to helping the brand accomplish specific outcomes, simple screenshots are unlikely to tell the whole story.

Common mistakes and pitfalls during analysis.

- Not sending a "Post-Campaign Report" to the brand
- Assuming the brand is disappointed with the views/likes/opens/downloads/sales/attendees
- Not using comments & insights to pitch the next deal
- Not creating case studies to help you win new deals

Nelson Mandela famously said, "I never lose. I either win or learn."

When you ask a brand how they felt the campaign went, this must be your mindset.

Obviously, the best-case scenario would be for them to say, "It went awesome!"

Then you'd likely have zero hesitation pitching them on the next deal, right?

But if the brand says, "It didn't go well" or "It went average," your immediate response should be, "Thank you so much for letting me know. I have some ideas about why, but can you share *your* suspicions?"

Don't be surprised if the brand tells you about a *new* goal or objective they were measuring internally but never told you about.

A typical example is when a brand initially says it wants awareness then is disappointed the campaign didn't generate many sales.

In those situations, you must explain that there was a misalignment of tactics and how you'll satisfy this newly identified goal in the next iteration (refer back to Chapter 2 section: "Pivot what you propose based on what you learn from the brand").

Your objectivity and humility will stand out from the typical partner who wants to point fingers at everyone but themselves.

Once you have an initial pulse check from the brand and compiled your data, it's time to assemble your Post-Campaign Report.

Create a "Post-Campaign Report" with your comprehensive analysis.

Brendan Gahan, former partner at advertising agency Mekanism, once told me, "I've worked on thousands of campaigns, and I've only had one creator put together slides and a report."

Remember: the bar is in the basement.

I don't know about you, but I'd prefer to live in a penthouse over a basement.

Think of the Post-Campaign Report (PCR) as your private elevator.

Post-Campaign Report Checklist

- ✓ **Overview**
- ✓ **Deliverables**
- ✓ **Key Insights**
- ✓ **Next Campaign Pitch**
- ✓ **Testimonial**
- ✓ **Data Appendix**

Let's review the six key ingredients:

1. Overview

Open the PCR by including a high-level summary of the campaign objectives. Since this document will likely be shared internally with brand stakeholders (or, if it's an agency, with their client), it's important to remind everyone what the goals were.

2. Deliverables

Provide an overview of the work you produced or executed. If you published online assets, include links to every post for easy reference.

3. Key Insights

This section includes your quantitative *and* qualitative analyses of how the campaign performed. Depending on the campaign goal(s), here are some ideas of what you could discuss:

Awareness

- Number of impressions or views relative to expectations
- Engagement rate relative to industry standards
- Screenshots of your audience saying they'd never heard of the brand, product, or event before

Repurposing

- Number or type of assets delivered relative to expectations
- Turnaround time relative to expectations
- Screenshots of your audience saying they saw your content or the ad

Conversion

- Number of sales/trials/downloads relative to expectations
- Click-through-rate (CTR) relative to industry standards
- Comparison to past campaigns or organic work you've published
- Screenshots of your audience saying they took action

Rack your brain to find creative ways to illustrate everything that was accomplished through this partnership.

Critically, you must share *all* results, including the positive *and* neutral/negative. An accurate analysis will not be possible if you ignore or sugarcoat obvious underperformance.

Remember how we proactively brainstormed objections your audience might have in Chapter 4 (Concept)?

It's time to compare those speculations to the public comments, private messages, or emails you may have received after the sponsorship.

Those neutral or negative insights can often become the focus of your next campaign pitch.

4. Next Campaign Pitch

When you pitch the brand on hiring you again, you should explicitly tie your proposal to the Key Insights.

If one part of the campaign overperformed, recommend doubling down on that for the next engagement.

If another part of the campaign received pushback, recommend either removing it *or* addressing it head-on if the objection is valid and significant.

If you're worried that it feels too soon to pitch them on a new campaign, remember the point of the pitch is not to get the deal immediately but to plant a seed in the brand's mind that you're ready and willing to re-engage.

5. Testimonial for *them*

Film a short video in which you share how much you enjoyed working with their team. Include details such as how seamless the experience was, how professional they were, or how much the campaign resonated with your audience.

Trust me, your video will be immediately shared with everyone internally or forwarded to the client.

We've had our testimonials played during "All-Hands" meetings, where the entire brand, including the executive team, saw them!

What do you think will happen the next time they plan a campaign?

The VP of Marketing will tell the Partnerships team, *"Make sure to re-hire those creators that made us that testimonial a few months ago."*

6. Data Appendix

The final section of the PCR is the Appendix, where you can include all the analytics screenshots your heart desires.

This information is at the end rather than the beginning because you want to keep the focus on your holistic insights.

And if the brand needs the raw numbers for their internal reporting, they're easily accessible.

The prospect of putting together a Post-Campaign Report may feel overwhelming.

But remember, *the very act of submitting a PCR* will differentiate you from every other partner they hired.

To hammer this home: Molly Donlan, one of my students, told me, *"The Post-Campaign Report is GOLD. Brands are always so impressed by them and often offer a second deal from that alone."*

Stay top of mind by sending the brand ongoing value.

Don't be surprised if the brand doesn't immediately say, "Yes!" to your next campaign proposal.

There may be several reasons why they can't move forward right away, such as budget constraints, additional meetings they need to have, or shifting priorities.

But the last thing you should do is never talk to them again!

That's like firing yourself from your 9-5 job *every month* and constantly having to find a new one.

Do you know how much easier it is to convince a company you did great work with to hire you again (when they're ready)?

The key to stop doing business (and life) on "hard mode" is to stay top of mind by sending ongoing, valuable updates.

Don't simply spam the brand with gems like: "Bringing this to the top of your inbox!" or "Just circling back!" Linguists across the globe have tried creating a more irritating sequence of words than these but none have succeeded.

Don't be that person. Instead, use what I call the "P.I.N.O.T. Method":

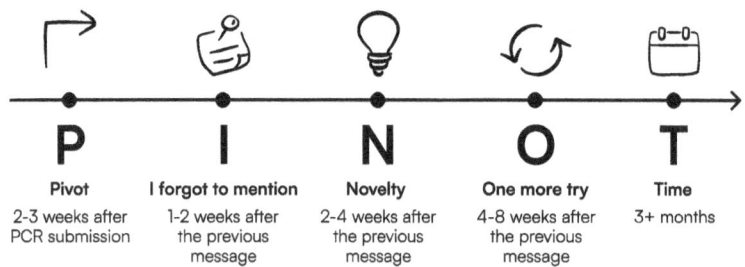

P	**I**	**N**	**O**	**T**
Pivot	I forgot to mention	Novelty	One more try	Time
2-3 weeks after PCR submission	1-2 weeks after the previous message	2-4 weeks after the previous message	4-8 weeks after the previous message	3+ months

Here's what you can say each time you reach out:

Pivot (Follow-up #1; 2-3 weeks after PCR submission)

Thank the brand for the payment you just received and ask
for feedback on the next campaign idea you submitted in the
Post-Campaign Report

- Send the brand a new seasonal idea ("Instead of a summer
  campaign, how about Back-to-School? Not feeling Back-to-
  School? How about for the holidays?")
- Send the brand a new idea related to their recent post (I
  hope you turned on notifications for their social media
  accounts!)
- Send the brand a new idea related to additional feedback/
  comments you got from the audience on the first campaign.
- Send the brand a new idea related to a trend ("Check out
  this article I saw about how this brand in your category is
  killing it with short-form content!")
- Tell the brand about other distribution channels you have
  ("I know we worked together on platform X, but have you
  considered platform Y?")

**I forgot to mention (Follow-up #2; 1-2 weeks after the
previous message)**

- *"I forgot to mention that our post has continued to do well!
  Since we last spoke, it's gotten X more views, impressions,
  and downloads!"*
- *"I forgot to mention that my calendar is filling up for the
  season, and I have two more slots for fall..."*
- *"I forgot to mention if my last idea didn't resonate, here's
  another..."*
- *"I forgot to mention I can also create exclusive content for
  your social handles..."*
- *"I forgot to mention I can also offer paid usage rights..."*

Novelty (Follow-up #3; 2-4 weeks after the previous message)

- *"Can you tell me what the brand's typical planning cycle looks like? I'd love to offer to do a virtual 'Lunch and Learn' with your marketing team where you can ask me anything, or best practices on platform Y, etc."*
- *"I noticed something about a few of the posts you made last week and would love to offer some tips for better engagement."*

One more try (Follow-up #4; 4-8 weeks after the previous message)

Review the approaches outlined in the previous three steps and try one more outreach using those tactics.

Let me pause here for a moment and acknowledge what you might be thinking:

> *"Justin, there's no way I'll ever find the confidence to follow up with a brand four times without hearing back from them."*

Well, let me share something one of my students, Emma, posted in my private community,

> *"The person I'm emailing just replied after the fourth email. You are so right to encourage people to keep going even if it feels uncomfy! They apologized for their late reply, and we're moving forward. Without you and Brand Deal Wizard, I would have 100% given up before."*

Of course, it's possible that after four emails, the brand still hasn't responded.

And if that's the case...

Time (Follow-up #5; 3+ months)

It's time to let your contact "breathe" for a few months.

For whatever reason (likely nothing to do with you), the brand isn't interested in a collaboration right now.

Set your calendar reminder for three months from now and then start the pitch process all over again.

Create case studies to land sponsorships with new brands.

While Post-Campaign Reports help you sell additional campaigns to brands you've already worked with, Case Studies help you sell campaigns to *new* brands you've never worked with.

Case Study Ingredients

→ Campaign goal
→ Brand details
→ Photos or screenshots
→ Statement of work
→ Behind-the-scenes facts
→ Results or performance
→ Testimonial and contact info

Let's review the seven key ingredients of a compelling case study:

1. Campaign goal

Make it clear whether this campaign focused on Awareness, Repurposing, or Conversion.

2. Brand details

Indicate the brand's name, add its logo, and what product or service you were promoting.

3. Photos or screenshots

Include prominent visuals with links to the published assets so the new brand can better understand how you helped bring the campaign to life.

4. Statement of work

List all the deliverables you produced for the partnership.

5. Behind-the-scenes facts

Think about all the under-the-radar things you did for the campaign that would impress a new brand. Here are a few examples I've included in the past:

"Turnaround from first contact to content delivery: 10 days."

"Revisions requested: 0"

6. Results or performance

Depending on the campaign goal, include relevant metrics that illustrate the partnership's success.

Here are a few examples I included in an Awareness campaign in the past:

"48,651 organic impressions"

"4.3% engagement rate"

"312 comments"

However, if the campaign goal differed (e.g., Conversion), you must include different metrics, like the number of sales generated.

Refer to the A.R.C. framework (Chapter 2) for the relevant Key Performance Indicators you should consider.

7. Testimonial and contact info

Finish off strong with a compelling quote from your brand or agency contact that lets the new brand know paying you a bunch of money is a safe investment.

Here's an example testimonial I've included in the past:

"Justin and April were an absolute pleasure to work with. They both displayed a killer work ethic and creative mindset, which helped bring to life social content that our clients were proud to share internally."

The new brand has to be chomping at the bit to work with you, right?

So, don't forget your contact information at the bottom.

Be smart with how you leverage case studies.

Imagine you're talking with a new brand and they tell you their objective is conversions.

What do you think their reaction will be when you send them an awareness-focused case study?

Confusion, most likely.

To get approval up the food chain, especially if you're asking for a lot of money, the brand needs resources to help them derisk the decision.

So, only send them case studies that align with their objective!

That way, they have air cover if things go south.

Here are my favorite ways to utilize case studies:
- When cold pitching: *"I have a case study I'd love to show you that seems relevant."* Critically, you're not sending it in the first email; only when you've identified their goal.
- When sending a proposal or pricing, say, *"Here are a few packages. Also, if it might be helpful, here's a case study from my recent partnership with Brand XYZ that had a similar goal."*
- Pin as a featured link on social media or your website
- Add to the front of your media kit. *Protip: Swap out the most relevant case study for that brand's industry or product category before sending it.*

My rule of thumb for how many case studies to create is *at least one per campaign goal type per content category.*

For example, if you're a fashion and home decor creator, aim for:

- One brand awareness-focused for fashion
- One brand awareness-focused for home decor
- One repurposing-focused for fashion
- One repurposing-focused for home decor
- One conversion-focused for fashion
- One conversion-focused for home decor

Awareness	Repurposing	Conversion
👕	👟	👜
🛋️	🪴	💡

That way, no matter the brand or the objective, you'll always have a relevant example of how you can serve them.

By the way, if you haven't done many sponsorships before, you can still create case studies by leveraging other types of performance data.

For example, if you have been an affiliate for a specific brand and can share how much revenue you've generated over the last 12 months, that will be compelling to a new brand with a conversion-focused goal.

Note: *You can access 10+ Case Study templates through my Brand Deal Wizard course:* **sponsormagnet.com/course**

You've now conducted a complete analysis with your Post-Campaign Report and created case studies to leverage for future pitches.

The last brand gets your PCR (with your next pitch) and a new brand gets your case studies (with a new pitch).

Do you know what this means?

You've just spun the Sponsorship Wheel!

And you can keep spinning it over and over and over to land consistent, well-paying sponsorships.

Bonus:

Claim the free bonus from this chapter

at ***sponsormagnet.com/analyze***

- P.I.N.O.T. method framework

Affirmations and Next Steps

You have come so, so far since picking up this book.

You set aside your hesitations and concerns. Suspended your disbelief. Opened your mind to a better, more abundant future for yourself and your business.

I'm proud of you.

You've learned what it takes to craft a pitch no brand will ignore.

You've learned how to properly negotiate so you stop leaving thousands on the table.

You've learned why carefully reviewing contracts is critical so you can protect yourself.

You've learned why you must send concepts to the brand in advance so you can avoid finger-pointing and busywork.

You've learned what it takes to produce top-tier work so brands marvel at your professionalism.

You've learned how to handle feedback objectively so your relationship with the brand is reinforced versus soured.

You've learned all the publication best practices so you don't screw up critical details at the last minute.

You've learned why conducting your own campaign analysis will differentiate you and allow you to pitch future partnerships.

But my most sincere hope is that the next time a brand comes knocking, you'll remember:

The knowledge you have and what you create is valuable.

Your instincts are good.

You do not work for free.

Educating brands can be a joy.

You are not just a creator, you're a consultant.

Brands are not your enemy.

The choices other creators make do not affect you.

You work with brands, not for them.

You do not need anyone's permission to pitch brands.

There is more than enough money to go around.

You are in control at all times.

Because you are a Sponsor Magnet.

Additional support and resources to make more money with sponsorships.

If you need help implementing the strategies from this book, visit *sponsormagnet.com/help*

Brand Deal Wizard (Course)

Brand Deal Wizard is an innovative, self-paced course revolutionizing the way content creators and influencers approach brand partnerships. This comprehensive program addresses a critical gap in the creator economy: the ability to secure lucrative, long-term sponsorships that provide stable income.

At its core, Brand Deal Wizard is about transformation. It takes creators on a journey from sporadic, undervalued brand deals to becoming confident, strategic partners who command premium rates. The course is structured around a holistic approach to sponsorships, covering everything from initial pitching to pricing to long-term relationship building.

What sets Brand Deal Wizard apart is its practical, action-oriented approach. Creators don't just learn theory; they gain access to a treasure trove of resources including customizable templates, rate calculators, and real-world case studies. These tools allow for immediate implementation of the strategies taught.

Brand Deal Wizard isn't just for those with massive followings. It caters to creators across the spectrum, including those with niche, highly engaged audiences. It also encourages creators to see themselves as valuable business partners rather than mere content producers.

In a landscape where only a small percentage of creators earn a full-time living, Brand Deal Wizard stands as a beacon of hope and a roadmap to success. It's not just about landing the next deal; it's about building a sustainable, profitable career.

Learn more about Brand Deal Wizard at *sponsormagnet.com/course*

Wizard's Guild (Coaching)

Wizard's Guild is a unique coaching service designed to directly support creators on an ongoing basis with their pitching, pricing, and sponsorship strategy. It offers a fresh alternative to traditional managers, agents, or brokers, helping creators navigate their deals while retaining 100% of their earnings.

Wizard's Guild operates on an asynchronous model (no live calls), providing flexibility for creators worldwide. Members can submit questions at any time and receive expert advice from Creator Wizard's team of sponsorship coaches twice weekly. This structure ensures prompt guidance without the constraints of time zones or conflicting schedules.

The impact of Wizard's Guild extends beyond immediate financial gains. It offers a fundamental shift in how creators perceive their value in the marketplace to build thriving, sustainable businesses.

Learn more about Wizard's Guild at *sponsormagnet.com/ coaching*

♦ ∩ ♦
Sponsorship Success Stories

How this niche podcaster works with billion-dollar brands.

When Paul Jamison started his lawn care business, he had no idea that it would turn into a podcast with hundreds of thousands of listeners and brands eager to buy ad space — but that's exactly what happened.

Paul is the voice and creator of the Green Industry Podcast, which covers the ins and outs of the lawn care and landscaping industry. These days, he can boast that he works with some of the most recognizable home improvement and lawn care brands in the world, such as Lowe's and John Deere.

While you could call him a pro now, that's not at all how things started out. The very first time Paul took a call from a brand that wanted to sponsor him, he first had to...find a shirt.

It was 2019, about a year after Paul had launched the podcast. A brand had reached out to have a call about a potential deal and that day Paul happened to be with friends by the pool.

"I thought my phone was going to ring at three o'clock with my first sponsor. So I'm sitting there, in my bathing suit, and I was telling my buddy, 'Yeah, dude, I got a sponsor,'" he recalls.

"I thought I was all that and a bag of chips."

Three o'clock came and went with no call. Worried it was actually a scam, he checked his email and realized it was supposed to be a video conference call. He scrambled to find a shirt and hopped on. He was late, but he still managed to land his first deal for $1,000.

"I just couldn't comprehend someone paying to be on my podcast," he says.

"I was so happy — I was doing cartwheels and backflips. That was the first time I made money like that as a creator."

He didn't know much about negotiating deals when he took that call and offered several packages for mid-roll ads. The brand ended up picking his biggest offer.

That was the first clue that he was in a stronger position to negotiate than he realized, but it would take a few years and a lot of coaching with Creator Wizard founder, Justin Moore, to realize just how much money he was leaving on the table.

From the Lawns of Atlanta to the Airwaves

Paul launched his lawn care business in Atlanta in 2011. The first few years, he says, were difficult. He even ended up working nights at a restaurant to make ends meet. But by 2017, things had turned around and Paul was growing his client base and making a profit. In 2018, he got the idea for his podcast because he wanted to share the story of his struggles starting out and how he was growing it into a sustainable small business.

"I just started cranking out podcast episodes, sharing my stories and my real-life experiences as a lawn care business operator and owner," he says. The Green Industry Podcast quickly became popular, cracking the top 100 in the business and entrepreneur-ship category. Paul realized even people who worked in different industries were tuning in to hear his tips as a business owner.

From there, he added Instagram, YouTube, TikTok, and Facebook to his portfolio, and suddenly he had a small media empire on his hands. He traveled to events and trade shows and interviewed lawn care industry leaders for the show. Soon, people were even recognizing him out in the world and asking for pictures and autographs. Yet, despite that massive success, it wasn't translating into money.

"We'd get all these views, all these downloads, all these likes, all these requests for pictures and autographs. But there's no money. What are we doing wrong?"

But a lightbulb moment was coming.

The Tools to Succeed

In those early deals, Paul worked out a less-than-ideal formula to figure out what to charge brands for sponsorships. He'd simply talk to friends and other creators and do a quick calculation. He figured if he had 5% of a friend's audience, he should be charging 5% of what they were able to make. It was a race to the bottom, and no one was winning.

That all changed when Paul heard Justin on a podcast.

"It was like a divine moment, so to speak," says Paul. Here was Justin answering all the questions Paul had been asking his friends, but with real answers.

Paul immediately started following Justin and watching his livestreams, and soon decided that coaching would absolutely be worth it.

"I felt like I was leaving more money on the table than what I had to pay him. If he can help me retrieve some of that money, it was going to be worth it," he says. And it was worth it. In their first session, it became crystal clear that Paul had been setting his prices too low, and that was a problem. Once you've set a low price precedent with a brand, it's hard to come back and command higher fees.

"I screwed things up with some of my favorite brands by offering my services for so cheap, and with a lot of deliverables," says Paul. "But thankfully, with all the new brand [deal flow] since working with Justin, we've been able to set some really good price precedence and healthy win-win sponsorships."

Together, they also identified and addressed one of Paul's weaknesses — emails with brands. Paul simply didn't know the lingo used to negotiate these deals, but Justin went through his inbox and helped Paul respond to brands with confidence and expertise. Paul was then able to use those communications like templates to talk to brands on his own.

Also vital to Paul was Justin's Sponsorship Wheel. This is Justin's eight-step process for working with any brand. It walks creators through the process from pitching, to negotiating, to creating the deliverables, to analyzing successes and failures to nurture an ongoing relationship with brands. These are the tools that set

Paul up for success, but it was only the beginning of his relationship with Creator Wizard.

A Coach in your Pocket

Paul is with Justin for the long haul. He's taken all of Creator Wizard's courses and is part of the Wizard's Guild coaching program.

With that ongoing relationship, Paul says Justin's team of sponsorship coaches are always there to help him navigate new terrain and new deals. It means that every time a new brand reaches out or Paul has a question, he knows he has help just a call away.

"It's just good to have somebody more well-versed in the sponsorship world double-check an email before I send it out to the brand," Paul says.

Paul says the return on investment in working with Justin has absolutely paid off — he's working with his dream brands and commanding more money per deal than ever before. It's even having a ripple effect — Paul keeps referring fellow creators to Justin because, in his words, "the rising tide raises all ships." When everyone is charging what they're worth, everyone wins.

It also begs the question — why choose a coaching service like Wizard's Guild over a sponsorship manager? For Paul, it's an easy choice.

"Managers ultimately don't have your best interest in mind," he says. The motivation for a manager is to get their cut of each deal, not to make the best deals possible for the creator. Ultimately, they're building up their own brand and reputation — not yours. In working with Justin's team of sponsorship coaches, Paul maintains complete control over his business and keeps 100%

of his sponsorship revenue. "What's helpful about Justin and his team is they give me the tools to represent myself. I'm able to talk to these brands and ultimately send out my proposals. They put me in the best position to win and to earn more money," Paul says.

Working with Brands, Not for Them

One of the most transformational strategies Paul has learned from working with Creator Wizard is how to approach his relationship with brands. He's no longer simply receiving instructions and following through; he's presenting himself as a partner. His goal is now to understand the brands he's working with — their marketing objectives, the audience they want to reach, and the best product he can offer for their goals. He knows there's not a one-size-fits-all solution.

Sometimes the brand's goal is to promote a trade show, sell a product, or reach a new audience. He now knows how to provide packages that can achieve those goals. He also has the confidence that he can give brands the best value for their money and outperform other marketing options like ad campaigns. He also learned from Justin to follow up all his campaigns with a report that shows the impact he generated, which leads to new deals with those brands.

"A lot of these brands I worked with a few years ago, when I started working with Justin, we [collaborated] again this year. And we're already talking about working again next year," he says. Part of the reason is that Paul now understands the power of his niche. Lawn care and landscaping may sound like it would bring limited opportunities, but the opposite is true. Paul has cultivated an audience with a lucrative focus who have a deep trust in Paul's expertise. And that has immense value.

"It's very eye-opening to me to see the power you have when you have a niche and the way you can convert your audience into customers of these companies. They see that and they're willing to pay for that," Paul says.

A Thriving Business on All Fronts

Paul has now moved to Florida and is focusing on content creation full-time. He still does landscaping when he has time, but "I've been enjoying the air conditioning for once in my life." Far from that first call when he was scrambling for a shirt, these days Paul is landing deals with major brands worth tens of thousands of dollars. He's living the dream of running multiple businesses including a successful podcast that more than pays the bills.

"I've been a creator — broke and busted — and I've been a creator making money. When you get to do what you love and you get to make a lot of money doing it, it's exhilarating. It's so much fun."

How this finance YouTuber scored her biggest sponsorship.

Jenny Hoyos grew up on YouTube. She first started posting content when she was just eight. In her big family, all her cousins had channels, so it only felt natural that she should, too.

She also happens to come from a family of entrepreneurs. Her parents had multiple businesses and the drive to scrape and hustle was instilled in her from a young age. So it should be no surprise that Jenny decided to take her YouTube more seriously and launch a channel all about personal finance.

She had all the right equipment and all the right ambition and quickly grew her channel, now boasting millions of subscribers.

Yet despite her massive success (and the topic of her channel even being money!), there was no blueprint for managing her own channel as a business. So when brands started reaching out to make deals, she was lost. "I literally knew nothing. I didn't know what to charge. I didn't know anything about contracts. I knew absolutely nothing when these people were reaching out to me," she says.

Jenny has always been scrappy, so she did her best to navigate the world of sponsorships. But everyone needs help sometimes.

From Hobby to Career

Although Jenny has been posting content for a decade, it was only recently that she found her niche. She noticed an uptick in interest in personal finance, so she focused on that theme.

The growth was, as she describes it, exponential. It took a year to get her first 1,000 subscribers, then it turned into 10,000 over a month...then 60,000...then 100,000...then 200,000...and on and on.

Many of those jumps in subscribers were spurred by viral videos. For example, Jenny posted a video of how to get a $3 burrito at Chipotle that blew up, got media coverage, and millions of views.

She continues to crank out viral videos about finding a $5 Christmas gift or gold in $20 of dirt. Jenny is even studying finance in college and runs her channel on top of being a student.

When Brands Came Calling

Given Jenny's skyrocketing numbers, it was only a matter of time before brands started reaching out with sponsorship deals. Although she used to get spammy offers, the real deals started coming in recently.

The problem is that it can be challenging to find information on how to negotiate brand deals. While some larger creators may release numbers now and then, she wished for a playbook for understanding benchmarks and how much to charge.

Jenny had a friend who was a fellow creator with a bit of experience negotiating brand deals. She would screenshot emails from brands and send them to him, and he'd do his best to offer advice on what to charge.

It helped her get by, but Jenny just knew she was leaving money on the table. "I undercharged myself so badly," she says. "It's almost embarrassing how much I was undercharging." She scoured the internet for resources, which led her to find Justin from Creator Wizard, and that's when everything changed.

Learning There's So Much to Learn

At first, Jenny was pretty sure she just needed help with pricing. But she quickly realized she needed help with...everything. She compared it to the "parabola of knowledge." When you first start learning a concept, you know nothing, but *you know* you know nothing. As you gain more knowledge, you start overestimating how much you know, putting you in the tricky spot of being overconfident in your abilities. Consuming Justin's content, she realized that's exactly where she was.

Jenny heard about Creator Wizard by the buzz Justin has built in the creator community. She had two friends who had worked with his team of sponsorship coaches and they suggested she check it out.

She finally reached out when a big offer landed in her inbox and she didn't know how to navigate it. It was more than just sponsored videos and involved creating original content for mainstream media. It was complex and new and Jenny didn't know what to do.

"I had a really big opportunity and I knew I didn't want to under-charge or negotiate improperly," she says. "I asked my friend for help and he was like, 'Oh, this is really complicated. This is beyond me. You need to reach out to Justin.'"

How Creator Wizard Changed Jenny's Business

After Jenny had her first consultation with Creator Wizard, it opened up a whole new world of possibilities. The first big lesson was to offer packages. It used to be that a brand would reach out and Jenny would just come up with a number. But that's almost never the best course of action.

She learned to offer a suite of packages that included not just YouTube videos but access to the audiences she's built on other short-form platforms. Rather than a one-off video, she can offer much more value and build a deal that includes multiple chan-nels and posts. That also lends itself to building long-lasting relationships with brands.

"Now when people reach out to me, I don't give my price imme-diately. I ask a bunch of questions to understand what they're looking for. *Then* I shoot them packages," she says. Jenny also learned that it's her job to understand the needs of the brands she's working with. She asks questions about their goals, their target audience, and their budget. Then she's able to craft a bespoke offer that's more enticing.

She went through her email offers with Justin line by line and said Justin has an amazing ability to understand those com-munications like a psychologist. "He was reading these people like a book, through their emails," says Jenny. For example, she learned that when a brand follows up very quickly, that's often a signal they really want to work with you and are anxious to get the partnership locked in.

As for that major deal, the brand originally wanted to do a trial run, but Justin swooped in. He advised Jenny to not only not do a trial but to offer a package of ten videos so there was a larger sample size to analyze what is (and what's not) working.

"Not only did we do 10x the amount of videos but he also increased the rate by double, which is actually nuts," she says. "I've also gotten $15,000 for a YouTube Short and it was literally a five-second integration."

Jenny Found Her Confidence

There was a time when Jenny felt so lucky to be getting sponsorship offers that rocking the boat by negotiating felt risky. But that's no longer the case.

"I would feel like, this brand is [huge] and I should be happy to work with them, even for free. But no...it shouldn't work like that," she says. Jenny now knows her value. She knows she's offering brands a connection to a large and loyal audience and that her financial expertise makes her a great partner. Especially after consuming Justin's resources, she knows that even smaller creators with fewer followers can land huge deals.

She also knows exactly how to illustrate her value proposition to brands, like having case studies on hand to display her expertise. In those case studies, she documents her biggest deals and how they performed — like the engagement or conversions. She's also started to see herself not as a run-of-the-mill influencer, but as a consultant.

"I [now] come to brands with a concept. I'll tell them how I'm gonna optimize it for retention and viewer satisfaction," she says.

"It depends on the audience you're serving and what value you can bring to the brand."

Investing in Yourself

Creators invest in themselves all the time, whether by buying new equipment or going on a trip to make new content. But Jenny says you need to think about the return on those investments.

For what she paid to work with Justin and his sponsorship coaches at Creator Wizard, Jenny has made that money back and much more.

"It's about investing in yourself in the areas that actually matter. For example, people say they're investing in themselves so they're going to pay $3,000 for a vacation because they're going to make a video off of it. That's not a good investment, because the return isn't great," she says.

Compare that to an investment that actually furthers your business and opens up your ability to make revenue...The choice is obvious.

How one brand deal paid this couple's mortgage for three years.

Troy and Shantel Brooks aren't just partners — they're *Spartners*. That's the word they use to describe their relationship as both spouses and business partners. Together they run a thriving lifestyle-based creator brand out of their home in the Atlanta area, incorporating family, faith, and fitness. They've gone from piecing together one-time deals to building long-term relationships with brands, which not only means secure income for their family but a vision for a career as creators.

Building their business to where it is now was a long road with a lot of trial and error, some major decisions for their family, and help from Justin at Creator Wizard to turn their brand into a full-time venture.

From Sweethearts to 'Spartners'

Troy and Shantel knew each other since seventh grade and kept in touch over the years through social media, although there were no sparks initially. In 2013, they were both living in New York City and Troy was working as a personal trainer while also creating content on the side. Shantel signed up for sessions and their second happened to fall on Valentine's Day. Clearly feeling a connection, they went out for drinks after their workout, and, in their own words, the rest is history. They were engaged nine months later and married nine months after that.

By then, Troy had already built a brand on social media as a fitness and lifestyle creator, scoring deals with high-profile brands like Lululemon. Eventually they made the move to Georgia, and although Troy's brand was thriving, Shantel wasn't ready to go all in. She had left a high-powered job in New York and wanted to start her own thing (but didn't know what that would be).

"She's like, 'I'm not going to stop doing what I'm doing to help you with your little social media influencer career. I'm an Ivy League grad, I'm a boss,'" says Troy. Shantel said she could see what Troy was doing was lucrative but readily admits she didn't take content creation seriously yet.

So she hustled — trying out different business ventures on her own, but nothing stuck. They looked at their schedules and could see their time together growing sparse. "We had very divided, isolated schedules. It reminded me of when I worked all day outside of the home and left him with our son. I missed out on so many moments and refused to allow that to happen again," says Shantel.

All this time, she had been helping Troy here and there with things like photography and Troy could see that collaborating with his wife was only making his brand and work stronger.

Shantel finally said, "I've been so focused on trying to do me and my thing, which has led to isolation, when I could just change my perspective, listen to him, and do *our* thing. I finally got past my ego, and was like, let me try this partnership thing with my husband. Our lives changed, and we officially became business partners."

Leveling up Their Sponsorship Game

Now a family man with two kids and a dog, Troy had moved his brand away from a focus on fitness to a focus on lifestyle and family. That came from changes in Troy's own life and perspectives, but it was also a savvy business move. Broadening his content also meant broadening the range of brands he could work with.

Troy's sponsorships had been pretty simple up to that point. He had moved past accepting free products for posts and was earning a little money for collaborations. But it was all very one-sided.

The first big eye-opener was when a personal training client, an entertainment lawyer, offered to look over his sponsorship contracts. That's when he learned some important concepts like indemnification clauses and perpetuity. That gave him a leg up, but the deals were still inconsistent. Some months he'd have a bunch, some months he'd have none. Troy and Shantel were operating from a place where they waited for brands to come to them. They also hadn't learned to negotiate — if a brand offered too little, they'd simply say no and move along.

They were leaving money on the table, but that all changed when Troy and Shantel found Justin Moore, founder of Creator Wizard.

It started with the free Creator Wizard newsletter and all the deal vocabulary Troy started to learn. "That gave me the confidence and language to speak with brands in a different way," says Troy. He went from barely negotiating to using terms like "Key Performance Indicators." Brands were impressed.

"Justin equipped us very early on with stuff to change the dynamic in regards to knowing it's not just a one-sided relationship," says Troy. Then it all came together when they signed up for Justin's Brand Deal Wizard course.

The Creator Wizard Transformation

When Troy and Shantel felt their business was growing stagnant, the Brand Deal Wizard course breathed new life into their venture as Spartners. "Justin's course was literally one of the best investments we've ever made into our content creation business," says Shantel. "It really equipped us with the right tools and strategy to pitch people."

That was the first big lesson — knowing their own strengths and learning how to proactively communicate those strengths to brands. They weren't just some creators accepting deals; they became a powerhouse that offered value to brands. They don't just offer exposure to their audience — they offer professionalism, dependability, and an understanding of how sponsorship deals benefit both parties. They went from offering simple rate cards to treating each deal as a bespoke arrangement. What are the usage rights? How many reshoots are included? What are the exclusivity terms? All these questions determined the exact parameters of every deal and how much they'd ultimately charge.

They also don't just walk away anymore. If a brand comes in too low, Troy and Shantel know how to communicate their value and expertise to command a better offer. All that has added up to more than $500,000 in sponsorship income, but most importantly, a renewed sense of confidence in their worth.

Troy and Shantel's Future

The biggest transformation for Troy and Shantel is that they now see themselves as partners to the brands they work with. "A partnership is more than a one-off," says Troy. "It's establishing real long-term partnerships with brands and being able to show them a multitude of things you can offer." That mindset and strategy has not only led to lucrative deals but also to new opportunities like consulting for brands. The future is very bright for Troy & Shantel, and they attribute a big part of their sponsorship success to Justin and his team at Creator Wizard.

Note: If you want to achieve the same sponsorship success as Paul, Jenny, Troy & Shantel, and hundreds of other students, you can access additional education and coaching at sponsormagnet.com/help

AND DON'T FORGET:

If this book helped you, it would mean the world to me if you took 60 seconds to write a quick review.

Simply visit *sponsormagnet.com/review*

Acknowledgements

I want to take this opportunity to thank the following people who have supported me along this journey.

April: My wife, my soul mate, my best friend. For having the guts and vision to start a YouTube channel in 2009. For letting me come along for the ride. I would have never learned any of this stuff were it not for the business you started. For supporting me through all my crazy entrepreneurial ups and downs. For being a nurturing, loving, and patient mom to our boys. For always being ready for our next adventure together. I love you always and forever.

Liam: My life changed the first time I held you in my arms. Watching you grow into a kind, curious, and confident boy makes me so proud to be your dad.

Jacob: My life changed again when I held you in my arms. Watching you grow into a funny, clever, and competitive boy makes me so proud to be your dad.

My dad, David: For always telling me I could accomplish absolutely anything. I'm proud to be your son.

My mom, Sharon: For always tearing up whenever I play the piano. I'm proud to be your son.

My stepmom, Susan: For loving me as if I were your own son when I needed it most.

My stepdad, Steve: For caring for my kids as though they were your own grandkids.

My sister, Jessica: For always being there for me growing up.

Dee Brissett: For being my counterbalance and helping turn Creator Wizard into a real business.

Russ Vasquez: For helping the business grow behind-the-scenes.

Bianca Wesang: For helping me finally balance my work with my life.

Joe Casabona: For supporting our community and for your comedic timing.

George Blackman: For helping ensure this book was funnier and easier to read.

Lauren Strapagiel: For interviewing my students and writing incredible success stories.

Jay Clouse: For inspiring me to think smarter and bigger.

Peter Hollens: For building me up when I doubted myself.

Alex Llull: For helping put Creator Wizard on the map.

Gil Kruger: For being the only manager I don't tell creators to fire.

KC Procter: For helping ensure this book impacts as many people as possible.

Rob Freund: For verifying the accuracy and completeness of the Contract chapter.

Roberto Blake, Nick Nimmin, Daniel Batal, Sean Cannell, and Benji Travis: For inspiring me to help educate the next generation of creators.

Dorothy Ilson, Jim Hamilton, John Lawson, and Darrell Vesterfelt: For helping make my business more stable.

Kevin Herrera: For being such a vocal advocate.

Mike Pacchione: For helping me articulate my ideas so I don't sound like an idiot.

All of my beta readers, especially Milo aka MrRoflWaffles: For sending me thirty-minute voice notes that helped shape the book's tone early on.

Charlotte Crowther: For helping codify my Sponsorship Wheel methodology.

Joshua Lisec: For helping with an early outline of this book.

Dale Roberts: For giving me the confidence to self-publish.

Pat Flynn: For telling me to ignore the sunk-cost fallacy.

Steven Pressfield: For helping me overcome Resistance.

Daniel Priestley: For helping me become a Key Person of Influence.

Derek Sivers: For helping me realize what's worth doing.

Sara Loretta and Martin Cris: For making Creator Wizard look like an actual business.

Rudy Montilla Torres, KC Procter, Mitchell Cohen, Martin Pratt, Kyle Balmer, David Liu, Owen Shrock, Dirgantara Fasa, Parker Hallberg, Aleksandra Zuraw, Delila Rodriguez, Jason Vaughn, Brian MacDuf, Tanja Kropf, Stuart Leslie, Katie Allred, Misha Larson, Rory Bland, Hector Carrasco, Dylan Bridger, Tim Enalls, Lew Smith, Justine Galea, Jeff Gargas, Chenell Basilio, Joshua Timothy, Jenny Lu, Lex Roman, Anthony Ross, Liron Segev, Chapo Ailurophile, Dom Kent, and Krystal Proffitt: For pre-ordering my book sight unseen.

Most importantly, all my students and clients: For allowing me to serve you.

About the Author

Justin Moore is a Sponsorship Coach & the founder of Creator Wizard, a school & community that teaches you how to find & negotiate your dream brand partnerships so you stop leaving thousands on the table.

Along with his wife April, Justin has been a full-time creator since 2014 and has personally made over $5M working with brands. He also ran an influencer marketing agency for seven years that helped other creators earn millions more.

Justin brings a very unique perspective because not only has he been a creator in the trenches doing sponsorships for years but, by running an agency, he has insider knowledge behind how big brands choose which influencers to partner with and why they pass on others.

Justin is so passionate about helping creators understand their worth that he shut down his agency to focus exclusively on educating, coaching, and writing about sponsorship strategy. His mission is to enable creators big and small to land 1 million paid brand partnerships in the next 10 years.

Learn more at *creatorwizard.com*